外贸函电

唐 伟 杨明远 主 编

中国财经出版传媒集团
经济科学出版社
Economic Science Press

图书在版编目（CIP）数据

外贸函电／唐伟，杨明远主编 . —北京：经济科学出版社，2017.4

ISBN 978 – 7 – 5141 – 7929 – 3

Ⅰ. ①外… Ⅱ. ①唐… ②杨… Ⅲ. ①对外贸易 – 英语 – 电报信函 – 写作 – 高等职业教育 – 教材 Ⅳ. ①H315

中国版本图书馆 CIP 数据核字（2017）第 073537 号

责任编辑：白留杰　程新月
责任校对：刘　昕
责任印制：李　鹏

外贸函电

唐　伟　杨明远　主　编

经济科学出版社出版、发行　新华书店经销
社址：北京市海淀区阜成路甲 28 号　邮编：100142
教材分社电话：010 – 88191354　发行部电话：010 – 88191522
网址：www.esp.com.cn
电子邮箱：bailiujie518@126.com
天猫网店：经济科学出版社旗舰店
网址：http://jjkxcbs.tmall.com
北京密兴印刷有限公司印装
787×1092　16 开　12.5 印张　310000 字
2017 年 5 月第 1 版　2017 年 5 月第 1 次印刷
ISBN 978 – 7 – 5141 – 7929 – 3　定价：28.00 元
（图书出现印装问题，本社负责调换。电话：010 – 88191510）
（版权所有　侵权必究　举报电话：010 – 88191586
电子邮箱：dbts@esp.com.cn）

前　言

本书编者为高等职业院校教师，有丰富的教学和实践经验。通过总结和分析教学中发现的问题，结合外贸工作的新变化，我们对本书的编写进行了创新。

第一，紧密结合高等职业院校商务英语专业学生的英语水平和入职后相关工作岗位的实际需要，打破传统教材等量齐观的做法，对于不同外贸环节所涉及的知识点有所增删，如合同等环节仅简要介绍，不做教学要求，相应知识可通过课外阅读材料等形式来掌握。

第二，突破了传统外贸函电类书籍以外贸环节为序的编写模式，采用案例式的编写模式，完整再现某一商品进口或出口交易的全过程，将相关环节和知识点有机融入具体案例，便于学生从整体上认知整个外贸流程，自然掌握各个环节中相应的函电特点。

第三，以我国当前进出口贸易的主要商品种类和主要贸易伙伴为中心来设计案例，有助于学生全面了解我国外贸的基本情况。

第四，在传授函电知识的同时，加入对贸易伙伴所在国家或地区的商业文化背景知识介绍，有利于学生从社会、经济、文化的高度和广度深入认识外贸工作，进一步提升函电书写和涉外交往能力。

编者衷心希望，学生能够通过本书全面、系统地掌握外贸函电知识，为今后的实际工作打下坚实的基础。本教材旨在适应新形势下的外贸函电教学要求，期待专家学者对书中的缺点与不足之处批评指正，帮助我们在今后的教材编写和教学实践中更好地完成任务。

在编写过程中，我们还参阅了同行的有关书籍和资料，在此表示诚挚的谢意。

编者
2017.3

目　　录

第一部分　出口业务 1

    案例 1　向美国 Wilson & Wilson 公司出口服装 1
    案例 2　向英国 Tomtoy 公司出口圣诞礼品 21
    案例 3　向南非 Thompson 公司出口手机 41
    案例 4　向俄罗斯 Zukov 公司出口苹果 61
    案例 5　向印度尼西亚 Maluka 公司出口计算机 81

第二部分　进口业务 101

    案例 1　从法国 Lancelot 公司进口化妆品 101
    案例 2　从加拿大 Bernstein 公司进口木材 121
    案例 3　从韩国佑赫会社进口液晶显示屏 138
    案例 4　从日本 Yamanitzu 公司进口高级彩色复印机 151
    案例 5　从德国 Gutenberg 公司进口汽车发动机 166

资源库 181

    资源库 1　国际贸易常用保险简介 181
    资源库 2　国际贸易常用报价与付款方式 184
    资源库 3　国际贸易规范术语举要 186
    资源库 4　国际贸易重要港口要览 190

参考文献 194

第一部分　出口业务

案例 1　向美国 Wilson & Wilson 公司出口服装

商业背景设定：
出口商：元龙公司（Yuanlong Co.，），中国知名服装企业，计划拓展其美国市场，正在多方寻找合作伙伴。
公司地址：中国山东省东营市头道桥街 25 号
总经理：王大卫
主要产品：真丝服装

进口商：Wilson & Wilson，美国最大的中国服装进口商之一，与众多中国企业有着多年的合作关系，在中国商业伙伴中享有较高的声誉。
公司地址：221 Eastern Dr.，New York
董事长：拜伦·威尔逊（Bryant Wilson）

美国是中国服装最重要的出口目的国之一。作为美国的经济中心，纽约拥有众多有影响力的服装进口和销售公司。经过一系列的市场调研，元龙公司认为 Wilson 公司的运营理念和商业背景最符合其业务拓展的需要，因此与 Wilson 公司取得联系，希望能和对方建立起良好的合作关系。

学习情境 1：建交函
(Correspondence for Establishing Business Relations)

知识目标： 1. 全面掌握建交函写作的要领。
2. 学习建交函写作的常用词组、典型句式。
3. 学习建交函写作的专业术语。
4. 学习建交函写作的商务背景知识。

能力目标：1. 能够熟练运用本环节所学习的专业术语、常用词组、典型句式正确撰写建交函。
2. 掌握建交函写作所需要的相关商务背景知识。

任务：元龙公司总经理王大卫给 Wilson & Wilson 公司董事长威尔逊先生发出建交函，表达与对方合作的意愿，并且希望早日得到回复。

请就此撰写一封建交函。

要求如下：
1. 介绍本公司基本情况。
2. 表达合作意愿。

你可以借助资料库中的相关资料来撰写建交函。

范例：

Yuanlong Garments Co.
No. 25 Toudaoqiao Street,
Dongying Shandong
P. R. China
Jan. 20, 2015

Wilson & Wilson
221 Eastern Dr.
New York
USA

Dear Mr. Wilson,

We have got your name and address from your website. As a well-established Chinese garments corporation, we are keen to expand our foreign trade. As yet, we have no business contacts in America, and would be pleased to consider any business proposals you may have. Enclosed please find our latest illustrated catalogue, together with our latest price list and conditions of sales for your information and shall be pleased to deal with any specific enquiries you may have concerning any of our products.

Should you require any further details about our company, please do not hesitate to contact us.

We look forward to hearing from you in the near future.

Sincerely yours

Wang Dawei

General Manager

如何找到你的潜在客户？

如何及时、准确地寻找到你的潜在客户呢？如果你对某一家公司感兴趣，怎么获取相关的详细资料呢？通常你可以通过以下几个渠道来取得所需的信息：

银行
商业刊物
报纸、杂志或广播电视上的广告
请你的商业伙伴推荐
市场调研
商务参赞办公室
行业协会
境内外的商会组织
向国外的商会求助

当然，目前最为便捷的方式就是网络，但是网络信息鱼龙混杂，要注意辨识虚伪的、诈骗性质的信息。

学习情境2：询盘函（Correspondence for Enquiry）

知识目标：1. 全面掌握询盘函写作的要领。
2. 学习询盘函的常用词组、典型句式。
3. 学习询盘函写作的专业术语。
4. 学习询盘函写作的商务背景知识。

能力目标：1. 能够熟练运用本环节所学习的专业术语、常用词组、典型句式正确撰写询盘函。
2. 掌握询盘函写作所需要的相关商务背景知识。

案例1 向美国 Wilson & Wilson 公司出口服装

任务： 在收到王大卫总经理的建交函后，威尔逊先生与公司董事会的成员进行了讨论。大家均认为这是一个非常好的机会，并委托威尔逊先生代表公司给王大卫总经理回函，对其来信表示感谢，同时希望元龙公司能寄送样品以供研究参考。

请就此撰写一封要求寄送样品的询盘函。

要求如下：
1. 感谢对方来电。
2. 要求寄送样品，长款红色、蓝色、黑色和绿色真丝围巾各一条。

你可以借助资料库中的相关资料来撰写询盘函。

范例：

Jan. 30, 2015

Dear Mr. Wang,

It is such a pleasure to have received your letter of Jan. 20, and we are very impressed by the wonderful design and beautiful coloring of your products.

Recently, there is a growing demand here for scarfs of high quality at our end, especially for the hand-made silk scarf. Although sales are not particularly high, good price can be obtained. Our requests are as follows: 100% silk, red, blue, black and green colors, size L. If your products are satisfactory, we are pleased to place an order with you.

We are looking forward to your favorable reply.

Sincerely yours

Wilson

任务： 威尔逊公司对于元龙公司寄来的围巾样品的质量非常满意，希望能与其开展贸易活动。威尔逊先生致函王大卫总经理，告知对方计划首批购买3000条长款红色真丝围巾，要求元龙公司进行报价。

请就此撰写一封要求报价的询盘函。

要求如下：

1. 对寄送样品表示满意。
2. 告知对方计划订购3000条红色围巾。
3. 请求元龙公司对此进行报价。

你可以借助资料库中的相关资料来撰写询盘函。

范例：

Feb. 20, 2015

Dear Mr. Wang,

We are in receipt of your samples with many thanks and I am pleased to inform you that we are very satisfied with your products. To start the business, we are thinking of placing an order of 3000 long red scarfs and we would be grateful if you could quote us the details of your price and terms of payment. Should your price and quality be found competitive, we are sure much larger orders and the long-standing business and relationship between us will definitely follow.

We look forward to hearing from you soon.

Sincerely yours

Wilson

学习情境3：发盘函（Correspondence for Offers）

知识目标：1. 全面掌握发盘函写作的要领。
2. 学习发盘函写作的常用词组、典型句式。
3. 学习发盘函写作的专业术语。
4. 学习发盘函写作的商务背景知识。

能力目标： 1. 能够熟练运用本环节所学习的专业术语、常用词组、典型句式正确撰写发盘函。

2. 掌握发盘函写作所需要的相关商务背景知识。

任务： 收到威尔逊先生的询价信后，元龙公司认为这家公司是非常理想的合作伙伴，因此给它一个详细的发盘。

请就此撰写一封发盘函。

要求如下：

品名：100% silk scarfs
颜色：红色
尺码：长款
单价：每条35美元，CIF 纽约
数量：3000条
包装：牛皮纸箱，100条装入一箱
交货期：收到信用证后3周内发货
保险：由买方投保
支付方式：不可撤销的见票即付信用证

你可以借助资料库中的相关资料来撰写发盘函。

范例：

Mar. 10, 2015

Dear Mr. Wilson,

We have received your letter dated Nov. 30 and this is to make you firm offers for our silk scarfs.

  Commodity：100% silk scarfs
  Color：red
  Size：L
  Price：US＄35/pc, CIFNY
  Quantity：3000 pcs

Packing: 100 pieces in a brown paper box
Shipment: within 3 weeks of receiving L/C
Insurance: to be covered by the buyer
Terms of Payment: by confirmed, irrevocable L/C by draft at sight

We believe this price would be very competitive at your market and your early decision would be appreciated.

Yours faithfully

Wang Danwei

学习情境4：还盘函（Correspondence for Counter-offers）

知识目标：1. 全面掌握还盘函写作的要领。
2. 学习还盘函写作的常用词组、典型句式。
3. 学习还盘函写作的专业术语。
4. 学习还盘函写作的商务背景知识。

能力目标：1. 能够熟练运用本环节所学习的专业术语、常用词组、典型句式正确撰写还盘函。
2. 掌握还盘函写作所需要的相关商务背景知识。

任务：威尔逊公司收到元龙公司的报价后认为价格有些偏高，因此致函王大卫总经理，希望能得到优惠折扣。
请就此撰写一封还盘函。
要求如下：
1. 表示元龙公司报价偏高。
2. 说明来自越南、泰国等地的产品正充斥美国市场。
3. 要求得到10%的优惠折扣。

你可以借助资料库中的相关资料来撰写还盘函。

范例：

Mar. 21, 2015

案例1　向美国 Wilson & Wilson 公司出口服装

Dear Mr. Wang,

We have received your offer of Dec. 30 offering us 3000 scarfs at $35 each one and we regret to say that we find your price rather high and we believe we'll have a hard time convincing our clients at your price. You may have known that similar products from countries like Vietnam and Thailand are gushing into our market. Should you be ready to reduce your price by 10% we might come to business. We hope you will consider our counter-offer most favorable and let us know your decision as soon as possible.

Yours faithfully

Wilson

任务：元龙公司收到了威尔逊公司的还盘函，管理层经过测算后认为对方的还价超过了公司的预期，但是考虑到今后进一步合作的需要以及美国市场的巨大潜力，元龙公司最后决定，如果威尔逊公司的订货量超过5000条，则同意给与对方10%的折扣。
请就此撰写一封还盘函。
要求如下：
1. 对威尔逊公司未能接受己方的报价表示遗憾。
2. 强调自己产品的竞争优势。
3. 表示如果威尔逊公司的订货量超过5000条，则同意给与10%的折扣。

你可以借助资料库中的相关资料来撰写还盘函。

范例：

Dear Mr. Wilson,

Thank you for your letter and we are indeed sorry that you found our price too high. Actually the price we quoted is very favorable. I believe a comparison of the quality between our products and those from Vietnam and Thailand will convince you of the fairness of our quotation.

However, in view of our future cooperation, we have decided to give you an exceptional discount of 10 percent if your order reaches or exceeds 5000.

Yours faithfully

Wang Dawei

学习情境5：订单函（Correspondence for Orders）

知识目标： 1. 全面掌握订单函写作的要领。
2. 学习订单函写作的常用词组、典型句式。
3. 学习订单函写作的专业术语。
4. 学习订单函写作的商务背景知识。

能力目标： 1. 能够熟练运用本环节所学习的专业术语、常用词组、典型句式正确撰写订单函。
2. 掌握订单函写作所需要的相关商务背景知识。

任务： 收到元龙公司的报价后，威尔逊公司认真研究了相关条款，认为这份报价是合理的，因此决定和元龙公司进行交易，首批订购6000条围巾。
请就此撰写一封订单函。
要求如下：
1. 订购6000条长款红色丝巾。
2. 每条35美元，FOB天津。
3. 牛皮纸箱，100条装入一箱。
4. 收到信用证后3周内发货。
5. 保险由卖方投保。
6. 支付方式为不可撤销的见票即付信用证。
7. 强调货品品质须与样品一致。
8. 表示如首批订单令人满意则会继续合作。

你可以借助资料库中的相关资料来撰写订单函。

范例：

Apr. 10, 2015

Dear Mr. Wang,

We have received your letter dated Mar. 30. After considering your offers we take pleasure in placing an initial order with you for the following:

Commodity: Silk long red scarfs
Quantity: 6000
Packing: 100 sets in a brown paper box
Price: at US $35 each piece, FOB TianJin
Insurance: to be covered by the seller
Payment: by confirmed, irrevocable L/C by draft at sight
Shipment: within 3 weeks of receiving L/C

We would like to stress that the quality of your delivery should be in accordance with that of the samples you sent us and we will place bigger orders in the near future if the first order meets our demands.

Sincerely yours

Wilson

学习情境6：支付方式函（Correspondence for Terms of Payment）

知识目标：1. 全面掌握支付方式函写作的要领。
　　　　　2. 学习支付方式函写作的常用词组、典型句式。
　　　　　3. 学习支付方式函写作的专业术语。
　　　　　4. 学习支付方式函写作的商务背景知识。
能力目标：1. 能够熟练运用本环节所学习的专业术语、常用词组、典型句式正确撰写支付方式函。
　　　　　2. 掌握支付方式函写作所需要的相关商务背景知识。

任务：根据合同要求，威尔逊公司开立了信用证，并写信通知元龙公司。
请就此撰写一封开立信用证通知函。
要求如下：

1. 通知元龙公司根据双方签订的编号为 UHK – K009 的合同，B23536 号信用证已由运通银行纽约分行开出。
2. 金额为 21 万美元。
3. 信用证有效期截止到 2015 年 7 月 25 日。

你可以借助资料库中的相关资料来撰写开立信用证通知函。

范例：

April 25, 2015

Dear Mr. Wang Dawei,

RE: 6000 pcs of Red Silk Scarf under S/C No. UHK-K009

We'd like to inform you that L/C No. B23536 under the contract of UHK – K009 has been opened with Express Bank, New York for USD 210000. The L/C is valid until July 25, 2015. You will receive the above L/C very soon.

Yours faithfully

Wilson

任务：由于公司资金紧张以及银行利率提高，威尔逊公司认为继续使用原定的支付方式成本过高，因此希望能够对支付方式进行修改，以即期交单形式进行支付。
请就此撰写一封更改支付方式请求函。
要求如下：
1. 说明请求更改支付方式的原因。
2. 请求将支付方式更改为即期交单。

你可以借助资料库中的相关资料来撰写更改支付方式请求函。

范例：

Dear Mr. Wang,

Owing to the tight money condition and unprecedentedly high bank interests, we found paying by confirmed, irrevocable L/C really costs us a great deal and from the moment to open credit till the time our buyers pay us, the tie-up of our funds lasts over three months. So we would appreciate it if you would kindly make easier payment terms. We propose D/P at sight.

Your kindness in giving priority to the consideration of the above request and giving us an early reply will be highly appreciated.

Sincerely yours

Wilson

　　任务：收到威尔逊公司更改支付方式的请求函后，元龙公司对此进行了研究，认为当前世界货币市场非常不稳定，因此不能同意对方的请求。
　　请就此撰写一封不同意更改支付方式的回函。
　　要求如下：
　　1. 通知对方不能接受更改支付方式的请求。
　　2. 说明拒绝更改支付方式请求的理由。

你可以借助资料库中的相关资料来撰写回函。

范例：

Dear Mr. Wilson,

We are sorry to inform you that considering the unstableness of the current world monetary market, we cannot accept any terms of payment other than a L/C.

Yours faithfully

Wang Dawei

学习情境7：包装函（Correspondence for Packing）

知识目标：1. 全面掌握包装函写作的要领。
2. 学习包装函写作的常用词组、典型句式。
3. 学习包装函写作的专业术语。
4. 学习包装函写作的商务背景知识。

能力目标：1. 能够熟练运用本环节所学习的专业术语、常用词组、典型句式正确撰写包装函。
2. 掌握包装函写作所需要的相关商务背景知识。

任务：由于近期天气不佳、运输公司粗暴装卸等多种原因，威尔逊公司从中国客户处接收到的货物多次出现了包装受损的问题，在一定程度上影响了商品的销售。因此，在元龙公司的货物即将起运前，威尔逊公司认为有必要再次强调包装的重要性。

请就此撰写一封包装指示函。

要求如下：
1. 解释一下近期出现的包装受损现象。
2. 强调包装，尤其是适合长途海运包装的重要性。
3. 建议将产品放置在塑料袋而非牛皮纸袋中，并且应该标注"保持干燥"的警示语。

你可以借助资料库中的相关资料来撰写包装指示函。

范例：

Dear Mr. Wang,

Due to various reasons, such as bad weather and rough handle by the steamship company, recently serious damage of the packing of the goods we import from China has been frequently reported and some of them are unsalable.

In order to avoid possible future trouble, we would like stress the importance of the seaworthy export packing which should be suitable for the long distance ocean transportation. Therefore, we strongly recommend that the scarfs should be packed in plastic bags instead of brown paper one. In addition, directive marks like KEEP DRY should also be indicated.

案例1 向美国 Wilson & Wilson 公司出口服装

We look forward to receiving your shipping advice.

Yours sincerely

Wilson

学习情境 8：保险函（Correspondence for Insurance）

知识目标： 1. 全面掌握保险函写作的要领。
2. 学习保险函写作的常用词组、典型句式。
3. 学习保险函写作的专业术语。
4. 学习保险函写作的商务背景知识。

能力目标： 1. 能够熟练运用本环节所学习的专业术语、常用词组、典型句式正确撰写保险函。
2. 掌握保险函写作所需要的相关商务背景知识。

任务： 元龙公司按照合同在规定时间内安排好货运事宜，现致信威尔逊公司，通知对方已经按照惯例为相关商品购买了保险。

请就此撰写一封告之买方购买保险的通知函。

要求如下：

1. 告知对方已安排好运输事宜，货物将由"常青号"货轮承运。启运时间为 8 月 15 日。

2. 告知对方已经为商品投保发票金额 110% 的一切险。

你可以借助资料库中的相关资料来撰写保险函。

范例：

July 10, 2016

Dear Mr. Wilson,

RE：Insurance Covering S/C No. UHK-K009 for 6000 Silk Scarfs.

I am writing to inform you that we have book shipping space for the consignment on S. S. Evergreen which sails for New York on August 15.

We are also glad to tell you that we have covered insurance on the scarfs against All Risks for 110% of the invoice value.

Your prompt confirmation would be appreciated.

Yours sincerely

Wang Dawei

学习情境9：运输函（Correspondence for Shipment）

知识目标： 1. 全面掌握运输函写作的要领。
2. 学习运输函写作的常用词组、典型句式。
3. 学习运输函写作的专业术语。
4. 学习运输函写作的商务背景知识。

能力目标： 1. 能够熟练运用本环节所学习的专业术语、常用词组、典型句式正确撰写运输函。
2. 掌握运输函写作所需要的相关商务背景知识。

任务： 元龙公司获悉由于近期天气恶劣，严重影响了港口装运工作的正常进行，"常青号"的起航时间也因此被推迟到8月30日。
请就此撰写一封告知对方起运时间推迟的通知函。
要求如下：
1. 告知对方起运时间推迟的原因。
2. 告知对方启运时间推迟到8月30日。
3. 告知对方鉴于前期已预留了足够的时间余量，因此可以保证不会逾期交货。

你可以借助资料库中的相关资料来撰写通知函。

范例：

July 20, 2016

Dear Mr. Wilson,

We refer to our S/C No. UHK-K009 for 6000 silk scarfs due to be shipped on August 15.

Owing to the poor weather, the port could not operate normally recently. We are sorry learn that the S.S. Evergreen will not leave the port until August 30.

We believe, however, that the delivery deadline will still be met since enough time margins have been considered when we decided the previous shipping date.

We apologize for any inconvenience, but this delay is truly due to circumstances beyond our control.

Sincerely yours

Wang Dawei

学习情境10：索赔和纠纷解决（Correspondence for Claim and Settlement）

知识目标：1. 全面掌握索赔函写作的要领。
2. 学习索赔函写作的常用词组、典型句式。
3. 学习索赔函写作的专业术语。
4. 学习索赔函写作的商务背景知识。

能力目标：1. 能够熟练运用本环节所学习的专业术语、常用词组、典型句式正确撰写索赔函。
2. 掌握索赔函写作所需要的相关商务背景知识。

任务：经过1个多月的长途海运，威尔逊公司订购的货物终于到达了纽约。但是经过检验，威尔逊公司发现货物包装出现了问题，有可能影响产品销售。
请就此撰写一封索赔函。
要求如下：
1. 告知元龙公司货物已收到。
2. 告知元龙公司发现三箱货物包装破损，围巾无法销售，提出索赔。

你可以借助资料库中的相关资料来撰写索赔函。

范例：

Oct. 10, 2016

Dear Mr. Wang Dawei,

We regret to inform you that the 60 cartons of scarfs you shipped in New York on 30th August, 3 were badly damaged and the scarfs in them were dirty and practically unsalable, which of course we understand is not your fault. But we have to write to you to lodge a claim for 300 pieces of damaged scarf.

Enclosed is our quality inspection report and we should be grateful if you let us promptly have your opinions about these requirements.

Yours respectfully

Wilson

任务：经过与船运公司的紧急沟通和进一步调查，元龙公司致函威尔逊公司，告知其调查结果和公司对于索赔的建议。
请就此撰写一封索赔回复函。
要求如下：
1. 告知威尔逊公司，经过调查，元龙公司的包装完全符合相关要求，包装受损系因船运公司搬运不当所致。
2. 建议威尔逊公司向保险公司提出索赔。

你可以借助资料库中的相关资料来撰写索赔回复函。

范例：

Oct. 25, 2016

Dear Mr. Wilson,

RE: 3 Cartons of Damaged Silk Scarf

After serious investigation, we found that the scarfs were packed properly in accordance with the packaging requirements agreed by both parties. We have sufficient evidence to prove that the problem was caused by rough handle in transit.

Therefore we suggest that you should lodge your claim with the insurance company.

Sincerely yours

Wang Dawei

商业背景知识拓展

1. Introduction of American Economy

The United States of America is the world's biggest economy which makes up approximately 17 to 22 percent of the world's gross domestic product (GDP). The currency of the United States, the dollar, is the most widely used currency in international trade, as well as the world's foremost reserve currency.

Both private interests and state interventionism play important roles in the US economy. The US economy benefits from the country's rich natural resources, strong industrial and agricultural production, well-developed service industry, as well as extremely high rates of research, innovation, and capital investment. Host to the largest and most influential financial market in the world, America boasts both the New York Stock Exchange (NYSE) and National Association of Securities Dealers Automated Quotations (NASDAQ). Consumer spending comprised 71% of the US economy in

2013, and the United States has the largest consumer market in the world. As a result, the US possesses not only the largest economy, but also one of the most stable in the world. The US is the second largest overall trading nation and the world's second largest manufactured goods producer. It is also the third largest producer of oil and natural gas. The US consistently ranks around ninth or tenth in the world for per capita GDP, and American workers have some of the highest average household incomes in the world.

America's overall position as the world's largest economy will likely remain so for a number of years, but the US government must focus on improving aging infrastructure and addressing issues related to over-burdened social welfare programs in order to maintain that position. The US economy will continue to shift towards an increasingly service based economy, thanks in large part to the proliferation of technology giants on US soil. As the intellectual development of many high-tech devices remains domesticated in the United States, the production of those devices usually occurs overseas, where production costs keep these devices more affordable to the average consumer.

2. U.S.-China Trade Is a Win-Win Game

Sino-U.S. trade and economic cooperation has generated huge and real benefits for both parties. Only balanced China-U.S. trade could bring about sustained development, mutual benefits, and a win-win relationship.

China-U.S. trade and economic relations include services and investment as well as goods. American companies have invested over \$62.2 billion in China and their profits amounted to nearly \$8 billion in 2008 alone. Good value-for-money, labor-intensive goods imported from China have helped keep the cost of living down for Americans. Without consumer goods from China, the U.S. price index would go up an extra two percentage points every year.

From 2004 to 2008, the U.S. surplus in services with China grew by a phenomenal 35.4% annually, dwarfing the growth in China's surplus in goods with the U.S. In 2008, the total sales of American goods in the Chinese market, including goods exported from the U. S. to China, amounted to $224.7 billion, close to the value of goods China exported to the U. S. in 2008, which stood at $252.3. The two countries were almost balanced in terms of sales after adjustment for value-adding freight and insurance fees.

The achievement of this goal rests not with restricting China's exports to the U. S. but with increasing U. S. exports to China. Many experts believe that the U. S., while implementing its strategy to boost exports, should relax its export control against China, and expand the export of competitive products to China. Both countries should vigorously oppose trade protectionism and expand the convergence of their interests in economic and trade cooperation. The two economies are highly complementary with huge potentials. As long as both countries approach the commercial relationship in a responsible manner, they will definitely be able to make it more stable and sound.

案例2 向英国 Tomtoy 公司出口圣诞礼品

商业背景设定：

出口商：喜运公司（Xiyun Co.,），中国知名玩具制造企业，致力于生产和销售各种玩具制品。

公司地址：中国浙江省温州市文华大街5号

总经理：刘云女士

主要产品：玩具

进口商：Tomtoy，英国知名的连锁玩具销售商，曾与多家中国玩具制造商合作，在中国商业伙伴中享有较高的声誉。

公司地址：639 Cambridge Street, London

董事长：肯·伍兹（Ken Woods）

作为知名的玩具制造企业，喜运公司始终致力于开发新的产品。公司通过大量的市场调查发现，目前电子类圣诞礼物已经逐渐成为欧美圣诞礼物市场的主流产品，因此针对英国市场的需求，开发出一款可通过 App 软件利用手机、计算机等进行远程操控的扫地机器人（Telecleaner）。通过英国销售商联合会的介绍，喜运公司认为 Tomtoy 公司符合其业务拓展的需要，因此与 Tomtoy 公司取得联系，希望能和对方建立起良好的合作关系。

学习情境1：建交函
(Correspondence for Establishing Business Relations)

知识目标： 1. 全面掌握建交函写作的要领。
2. 学习建交函写作的常用词组、典型句式。
3. 学习建交函写作的专业术语。
4. 学习建交函写作的商务背景知识。

能力目标： 1. 能够熟练运用本环节所学习的专业术语、常用词组、典型句式正确撰写建交函。
2. 掌握建交函写作所需要的相关商务背景知识。

任务： 喜运公司总经理刘云给 Tomtoy 公司董事长伍兹先生发出一封建交函，表达与对方合作的意愿，并且希望早日得到回复。

请就此撰写一封建交函。
要求如下：
1. 介绍本公司基本情况。
2. 表达合作意愿。

你可以借助资料库中的相关资料来撰写建交函。

范例：

Xiyun Garments Co.
No. 5 Wenhua Street,
Wenzhou, Zhejiang
P. R. China
Jan. 20, 2015

Tomtoy
639 Cambridge Street
London, UK

Dear Mr. Woods,

Your company has been recommended to us by British Toy Dealers' Associate and we are in hope of entering into business relations with you.

As one of the biggest Chinese manufacturers, we have developed a brand new auto cleaner called Telecleaner, which can be controlled through App software with mobile phone or computer. We are sure this new product will become very popular with the British customers.

To give you a more detailed idea of our product, we enclose the latest illustrated catalogue, together with our latest price list and conditions of sales for your information. If you are interested in this item, please tell us and we would give you our lowest quotations.

We are looking forward to your favorable reply.

Sincerely yours

Liu Yun

General Manager

学习情境2：询盘函（Correspondence for Enquiry）

知识目标：1. 全面掌握询盘函写作的要领。
2. 学习询盘函的常用词组、典型句式。
3. 学习询盘函写作的专业术语。
4. 学习询盘函写作的商务背景知识。

能力目标：1. 能够熟练运用本环节所学习的专业术语、常用词组、典型句式正确撰写询盘函。
2. 掌握询盘函写作所需要的相关商务背景知识。

任务：收到喜运公司希望开展合作的邮件后，Tomtoy管理层对此进行了认真的研究，均认为喜运公司是一家非常有实力的企业，并且相信他们开发的Telecleaner非常适合英国市场的需求，因此决定和喜运公司就产品的销售问题进行协商。伍兹先生代表公司给刘云总经理回函，对其来信表示感谢，同时希望喜运公司能寄送样品以供客户反应测试。

请就此撰写一封要求寄送样品的询盘函。
要求如下：
1. 感谢对方来电。
2. 要求寄送样品，红色、蓝色、银色各5台以供客户反应调查之用。

你可以借助资料库中的相关资料来撰写询盘函。

范例：

Jan. 30, 2015
Dear Ms. Liu,

We are very pleased to receive your letter of Jan. 20, and your new product is very impressive. All of our sales staff believe it will become successful on this year's Christmas market if the quality can meet our standards and the price is reasonable.

We wonder if you could send us 5 samples for each color of red, blue and silver for the customer feedback survey and if your products are welcomed, we are pleased to place an order with you.

We are looking forward to your favorable reply.

Sincerely yours

Ken Woods

President

  任务：收到喜运公司寄来的扫地机器人样品后，Tomtoy 对它们进行了客户满意度测试，结果令公司非常满意，因此希望能从喜运公司订购产品。伍兹先生致函刘云总经理，告知对方计划首批购买蓝色、红色和银色机器人各 500 个，要求喜运公司进行报价。
  请就此撰写一封要求报价的询盘函。
  要求如下：
1. 对寄送样品表示满意。
2. 告知对方计划订购 1500 台机器人，红、蓝、银色各 500 台。
3. 请求喜运公司对此进行报价。

你可以借助资料库中的相关资料来撰写询盘函。

范例：

Feb. 20, 2015

Dear Ms. Liu,

We have received your samples and are happy to find that they are much better than we expected. Therefore, we would like to ask you to quote us the lowest CIF Liverpool for 1500 sets with 500 for red, blue and silver respectively. Please give us the details of your price and terms of payment.

Should we find your price and quality competitive, we shall place a large order with you.

We look forward to hearing from you soon.

Sincerely yours

Ken Woods

学习情境3：发盘函（Correspondence for Offers）

知识目标： 1. 全面掌握发盘函写作的要领。
2. 学习发盘函写作的常用词组、典型句式。
3. 学习发盘函写作的专业术语。
4. 学习发盘函写作的商务背景知识。

能力目标： 1. 能够熟练运用本环节所学习的专业术语、常用词组、典型句式正确撰写发盘函。
2. 掌握发盘函写作所需要的相关商务背景知识。

任务： 喜运公司收到了伍兹先生的询盘函，认为其购买意向是非常真实的，因此判断 Tomtoy 的确有意愿与之开展贸易活动，因此决定向其进行详细的发盘。
请就此撰写一封发盘函。
要求如下：
品名：Telecleaner 自动扫地机器人
颜色：红色、蓝色、银色
单价：每个30英镑，CIF 利物浦
数量：每种颜色500个，共计1500个
包装：木板箱，每箱100个
交货期：收到信用证后4周内发货
保险：由卖方投保
支付方式：不可撤销的见票即付信用证
此发盘有效期为7天。

案例2　向英国 Tomtoy 公司出口圣诞礼品

你可以借助资料库中的相关资料来撰写发盘函。

范例：

Mar. 10, 2015

Dear Mr. Woods,

We have received your letter dated Nov. 30 and this is to make you firm offers for our Telecleaners.

  Commodity: Telecleaner—Robotic Vacuum Cleaner
  Color: red, blue and silver
  Price: £30/set, CIF Liverpool
  Quantity: 500 sets for each color, 1500 sets in total
  Packing: 100 sets in a wooden pallet
  Shipment: within 4 weeks of receiving L/C
  Insurance: to be covered by the buyer
  Terms of Payment: by irrevocable L/C by draft at sight

We believe this price would be very competitive at your market and remind you that the offers are for 7 days.

Your early decision would be appreciated.

Yours faithfully

Ken Woods

学习情境4：还盘函（Correspondence for Counter-offers）

  知识目标：1. 全面掌握还盘函写作的要领。

2. 学习还盘函写作的常用词组、典型句式。
3. 学习还盘函写作的专业术语。
4. 学习还盘函写作的商务背景知识。

能力目标：1. 能够熟练运用本环节所学习的专业术语、常用词组、典型句式正确撰写还盘函。
2. 掌握还盘函写作所需要的相关商务背景知识。

任务：Tomtoy 收到喜运公司的报价后认为价格有些偏高，因此致函刘云总经理，希望能得到优惠折扣。

请就此撰写一封还盘函。

要求如下：
1. 表示喜运公司报价偏高。
2. 说明市场上有大量的类似产品，且价格均远低于喜运的报价。
3. 要求得到 20% 的优惠折扣。

你可以借助资料库中的相关资料来撰写还盘函。

范例：

Mar. 21, 2015

Dear Ms. Liu,

Your letter dated Mar. 10. offering us 1500 robotic cleaners at £30 each one has been received with many thanks. However, we are sorry to tell you our latest market survey shows the British market for e-cleaner is nowadays almost saturated with similar products at much lower price. We believe it will be very hard to convince our customers at your price and therefore, we are afraid we cannot come to business unless you reduce the price by 20%.

We believe this offer is in your best interests in the long run and your prompt reply will be highly appreciated.

Yours faithfully

Ken Woods

任务： 喜运公司对于 Tomtoy 的还盘函进行了研究，认为对方的还价超过了公司的承受能力，因此决定拒绝对方的还价请求。但是，为了今后的业务发展和双方的进一步合作，喜运公司承诺在今后的订单中会争取给与对方最优惠的价格。

请就此撰写一封还盘函。

要求如下：

1. 对 Tomtoy 公司未能接受己方的报价表示遗憾，表示无法降价。
2. 强调自己产品的竞争优势。
3. 表示今后的合作中会给予最优惠的价格。

你可以借助资料库中的相关资料来撰写还盘函。

范例：

Mar. 30, 2015

Dear Mr. Woods,

Thank you for your letter and we are indeed sorry that you found our price too high. Actually the price we quoted is very favorable since the recent soaring price of materials has seriously restricted our capacity for any price reduction. I believe the unique design and high quality of our products will eventually prove the fairness of our price.

However, in view of our future cooperation, we have decided to give you the most favorable and competitive offers in the future deals.

Yours faithfully
Liu Yun

学习情境 5：订单函（Correspondence for Orders）

知识目标： 1. 全面掌握订单函写作的要领。
     2. 学习订单函写作的常用词组、典型句式。

3. 学习订单函写作的专业术语。
4. 学习订单函写作的商务背景知识。

能力目标：1. 能够熟练运用本环节所学习的专业术语、常用词组、典型句式正确撰写订单函。
2. 掌握订单函写作所需要的相关商务背景知识。

任务：收到喜运公司的回复后，Tomtoy 重新进行了市场调研，认为其性价比的确有相当的优势，因此同意了喜运公司的报价，决定订购 1500 个机器人。

请就此撰写一封订单函。

要求如下：

1. 订购 1500 台扫地机器人，红色、蓝色、银色各 500 台。
2. 每台 30 英镑，CIF 利物浦。
3. 木板箱，50 台一箱。
4. 收到信用证后 4 周内发货。
5. 保险由卖方投保。
6. 支付方式为不可撤销的见票即付信用证。
7. 强调货品品质须与样品一致。
8. 表示如首批订单令人满意则会继续合作。

你可以借助资料库中的相关资料来撰写订单函。

范例：

April 10, 2015

Dear Ms. Liu,

We hereby inform you that after considering your offers we finally decide to place an initial order with you for the following.

  Commodity: Telecleaner—robotic vacuum cleaners
  Color: red, blue and silver
  Quantity: 500 sets for each color, 1500 sets in total
  Price: £30/set, CIF Liverpool
  Packing: 50 sets in a wooden pallet

Shipment: within 4 weeks of receiving L/C
Insurance: to be covered by the seller
Terms of Payment: by irrevocable L/C by draft at sight

We would like to stress that the quality of your delivery should be in accordance with that of the samples you sent us and we will place bigger orders in the near future if the first order meets our demands.

Sincerely yours

Ken Woods

学习情境6：支付方式函（Correspondence for Terms of Payment）

知识目标：1. 全面掌握支付方式函写作的要领。
2. 学习支付方式函写作的常用词组、典型句式。
3. 学习支付方式函写作的专业术语。
4. 学习支付方式函写作的商务背景知识。

能力目标：1. 能够熟练运用本环节所学习的专业术语、常用词组、典型句式正确撰写支付方式函。
2. 掌握支付方式函写作所需要的相关商务背景知识。

任务：根据前期的商谈结果，Tomtoy 和喜运公司签署了编号为 FFI-1354 号的销售合同。Tomtoy 按照合同要求按期在银行开立了信用证，并写信通知喜运公司。

请就此撰写一封开立信用证通知函。

要求如下：

1. 通知喜运公司根据双方签订的编号为 FFI-1354 的合同，SIF13335 号信用证已由英格兰皇家银行开立。

2. 金额为 45000 英镑。

3. 信用证有效期为 2015 年 10 月 20 日。

你可以借助资料库中的相关资料来撰写开立信用证通知函。

范例：

April 25, 2015

Dear Mr. Liu Yun,

RE: 1500 Sets of Robotic Vacuum Cleaner under S/C No. FFI – 1354

We'd like to inform you that L/C No. SIF13335 under the contract of FFI – 1354 has been opened with Royal Bank of England for 45000 pounds. The L/C is valid until 20 October, 2015. The L/C will be sent to you promptly.

Yours faithfully

Ken Woods

任务：当喜运公司开始紧张的生产和备货工作后，Tomtoy 公司却由于近期业务量剧增，资金流出现了暂时的紧张，因此希望对支付方式进行修改。

请就此撰写一封更改支付方式请求函。

要求如下：
1. 说明请求更改支付方式的原因。
2. 请求将支付方式更改为 30 天远期付款交单。

你可以借助资料库中的相关资料来撰写更改支付方式请求函。

范例：

May 10, 2015

Dear Ms. Liu,

Owing to the recent swift expansion, there is a temporary capital shortage. We are afraid the previously agreed payment term might hinder our capital flow. So we would appreciate it if you would kindly agree to D/P at 30 Days' Sight.

We are grateful if you could kindly consider this request.

Sincerely yours

Ken Woods

任务：收到 Tomtoy 的更改支付方式请求函后，喜运公司对此进行了研究。喜运公司认为 Tomtoy 作为英国最大的玩具进口商之一，有着较为良好的信誉。为了今后长期的合作，愿意做出一定的让步，因此建议货款的 50% 以信用证付款，另外的 50% 按即期付款交单方式结算。

请就此撰写一封同意更改支付方式的回函。
要求如下：
1. 通知对方不能完全接受更改支付方式的请求。
2. 说明建议的更改支付方式。

你可以借助资料库中的相关资料来撰写回函。

范例：

May 25, 2015

Dear Mr. Woods,

We are sorry to inform you that considering the unstableness of the current world monetary market, we cannot accept any terms of payment other than a L/C.

In order to conclude the business, we suggest that we meet half way by agreeing on 50% by L/C and the balance by D/P at sight.

Yours faithfully

Liu Yun

常用付款方式的风险分析：
L/C：Letter of Credit，信用证付款，这是国际贸易中最常用的付款方式。从理论上来说，L/C 是最安全、最保险的付款方式，因为它依托的是银行信用，而其他支付方式都是商业信用。

学习情境7：包装函（Correspondence for Packing）

知识目标： 1. 全面掌握包装函写作的要领。
2. 学习包装函写作的常用词组、典型句式。
3. 学习包装函写作的专业术语。
4. 学习包装函写作的商务背景知识。

能力目标： 1. 能够熟练运用本环节所学习的专业术语、常用词组、典型句式正确撰写包装函。
2. 掌握包装函写作所需要的相关商务背景知识。

任务： 由于电子产品在装卸、运输途中易于损害，Tomtoy 对于产品的包装工作非常重视，因此致信喜运公司，强调务必按照要求对产品进行认真的包装。
请就此撰写一封包装指示函。
要求如下：
1. 强调长途海运对于包装提出了较高的要求。
2. 要求每一台扫地机都要用防水布包裹。
3. 要求每 50 台扫地机放置于一个结实的木板箱中。
4. 要求标注"保持干燥"的警示语。

你可以借助资料库中的相关资料来撰写包装指示函。

范例：

Jun. 20, 2015

Dear Ms. Liu,

We are writing to stress the importance of proper packing to avoid any damages which will affect the future sales.

Taking in consideration of the hazards of marine transportation and the delicateness of the electronic device, we request you to cover every cleaner with waterproof cloth and place 50 sets into a strong wooden case. In addition, indicative mark like KEEP DRY should be shown clearly.

We look forward to hearing from you.

Yours sincerely

Ken Woods

学习情境8：保险函（Correspondence for Insurance）

知识目标： 1. 全面掌握保险函写作的要领。
2. 学习保险函写作的常用词组、典型句式。
3. 学习保险函写作的专业术语。
4. 学习保险函写作的商务背景知识。

能力目标： 1. 能够熟练运用本环节所学习的专业术语、常用词组、典型句式正确撰写保险函。
2. 掌握保险函写作所需要的相关商务背景知识。

任务：喜运公司按照合同在规定时间内安排好货运事宜，现致信Tomtoy，告知对方已为相关商品购买保险。

请就此撰写一封告知对方已购买保险的通知函。

要求如下：

1. 告知对方已安排好运输事宜，货物将由"华润号"货轮承运。启运时间为8月15日。

2. 告知对方为商品投保了平安险、水渍险和附加险。

你可以借助资料库中的相关资料来撰写保险函。

范例：

July 10, 2015

Dear Mr. Woods,

RE: Insurance Covering S/C No. FFI – 1354 for 1500 cleaners.

We are glad to inform you that we have book shipping space for the consignment on S.S. Huarun which sails for Liverpool on August 15. Moreover, we have arranged insurances covering F.P.A, W.P.A and Extraneous Risks.

If you have any further instructions, please do not hesitate to inform us.

Yours sincerely

Liu Yun

学习情境 9：运输函（Correspondence for Shipment）

知识目标：1. 全面掌握运输函写作的要领。
2. 学习运输函写作的常用词组、典型句式。
3. 学习运输函写作的专业术语。
4. 学习运输函写作的商务背景知识。

能力目标：1. 能够熟练运用本环节所学习的专业术语、常用词组、典型句式正确撰写运输函。
2. 掌握运输函写作所需要的相关商务背景知识。

任务：Tomtoy 发现市场上出现了越来越多的与喜运公司产品类似的扫地机器人。为了在即将来临的圣诞购物季的商战中取得佳绩，Tomtoy 希望喜运公司能提前完成货品的装运，将华润号的起航时间提前到 7 月 30 日。

请就此撰写一封请求对方起运时间提前的通知函。

要求如下：

1. 告知对方请求起运时间提前的原因和期望的日期。
2. 告知对方愿意承担这一改变所发生的合理费用。

你可以借助资料库中的相关资料来撰写通知函。

范例：

案例 2 向英国 Tomtoy 公司出口圣诞礼品

July 20, 2015

Dear Ms. Liu Yun,

We refer to the S/C No. FFI-1354 for 1500 cleaners due to be shipped on August 15. Our information proves that there are more and more similar products appearing on our market which we expect will continue to the traditional X-mas shopping season. To gain an edge for the likely fierce competition then, we hope the starting date of Huarun could be advance to July 30 and we will pay for any reasonable expenses generated by this change in date.

We apologize for any possible inconvenience, but we are sure this change will be mutually beneficial.

Sincerely yours

Liu Yun

学习情境 10：索赔和纠纷解决
(Correspondence for Claim and Settlement)

知识目标：1. 全面掌握索赔函写作的要领。
2. 学习索赔函写作的常用词组、典型句式。
3. 学习索赔函写作的专业术语。
4. 学习索赔函写作的商务背景知识。

能力目标：1. 能够熟练运用本环节所学习的专业术语、常用词组、典型句式正确撰写索赔函。
2. 掌握索赔函写作所需要的相关商务背景知识。

任务：经过喜运公司和轮船公司的通力合作，华润号终于提前起航，并在近1个月的长途海运后顺利抵达利物浦港。Tomtoy 验收货物时发现银色的机器人只有400台而非合同中要求的500台。

请就此撰写一封索赔函。

要求如下：

1. 告知喜运公司货物已收到。

2. 告知喜运公司发现银色机器人只有 400 台，提出索赔。

你可以借助资料库中的相关资料来撰写索赔函。

范例：

Aug. 30, 2015

Dear Mr. Liu Yun,

We have received the cleaners you shipped in Liverpool on July, 30. However, we regret to inform you that we found only 400 silver cleaners instead of 500 as stipulated in the sales contract, which we consider as a serious breach of the contract.

Enclosed is our quality inspection report and we should be grateful if you let us promptly have your opinions about these requirements.

Yours respectfully

Ken Woods

任务：经过与船运公司的紧急沟通和进一步调查，喜运公司致函 Tomtoy，告知其调查结果和公司的解决方案。
请就此撰写一封索赔回复函。
要求如下：
1. 告知 Tomtoy，经过公司调查，的确有 100 台银色机器人的箱子未被装上货轮。
2. 公司会立即将其通过空运直接送往伦敦，并承担相应费用。

你可以借助资料库中的相关资料来撰写索赔回复函。

范例：

Oct. 25, 2015

Dear Mr. Woods,

RE: Shortage of 100 Silver Cleaners

After serious investigation with the steamer company and port administration, we found that one wooden case with 100 silver cleaners had been left in the warehouse. We apologize sincerely for this huge mistake and have punished the staff concerned.

We have decided to send the cleaners by air freight directly to London a.s.a.p and the expense will be on our side.

Please accept our sincere apology and we guarantee that this will never happen again.

Sincerely yours

Liu Yun

数量短缺和提单案例

中国 X 电器设备出口公司与南美某国的 Y 外贸公司签订了一项关于某型电子设备的货物买卖合同。双方在合同中约定：由中国 X 公司作为卖方向 Y 公司出售一批电子设备，数量 50000 件，合同采用的贸易术语为 FOB 上海。双方还约定这批货物应在当年的 3 月 15 日前交付给 Y 公司指定的承运人。

3 月 9 日，中国 X 公司将生产好的 50000 件设备分别装在 1000 个纸箱中，交付 Y 公司指定的承运人——某远洋运输公司的"Z"轮进行运输。"Z"轮的船长在对这批货物进行了初步的检查以后，向中国 X 公司签发了清洁提单，并没有对这批货物从表面上看是否异常进行批注。中国 X 公司收到清洁提单后到银行议付了货款。

但是当这批设备运抵目的地后，Y 公司对这批货物进行了检查。结果发现这批货物并没有达到合同约定的数量 50000 件。在这 1000 个纸箱中有大约 100 余个纸箱出现了设备数量短少的情况，短少的数量从几件到几十件不等。Y 公司随后又立即请一家商品检验机构对这批货物进行了检验。这家商品检验机构也随即出具了有关这批货物数量短少的证明。鉴于此时中国 X 公司已经从银行议付了货款，Y 公司根据双方在买卖合同中签订的仲裁条款，向中国某国际经济贸易仲裁机构提交了仲裁申请。

中国 X 公司在收到仲裁通知以后，立即进行了答辩。中国 X 公司认为：首先，这批货物的承运人向该公司签发了清洁提单，说明这批货物在交付承运人的时候是完好的，不存在破损或数量短少的情况，因此不能证明数量短缺的责任在中国公司一方；第二，买卖双方在签订合同时约定的贸易术语是 FOB，根据该术语，货物由卖方交付承运人后，当货物跨过承运人的船舷时，货物灭失的风险就转移给了买方，作为卖方的中国 X 公司就不应为此承当任何责任，而作为买方的 Y 公司应当追究承运人——某远洋运输公司或有关的保险公司的责任；再次，Y 公司是在货物到达港口后才对这批货物进行了检验。中国 X 公司认为在该公司并未知晓的情况下，Y 公司就单方面对这批货物进行了检验，这对中国 X 公司来说是不公平的，检测的结果也是不能被接受的。

商业背景知识拓展

1. The Introduction of the British Economy

Great Britain has abundant supplies of coal, oil, and natural gas. Discovery of oil in the North Sea made it self-sufficient in petroleum. Other mineral resources include iron ore, tin, limestone, salt, china clay, oil shale, gypsum, and lead. Great Britain has achieved the position of one of the world's leading industrialized nations.

Within the manufacturing sector, the largest industries include machine tools; electric power, automation, and railroad equipment; ships; aircraft; motor vehicles and parts; electronic and communications equipment; metals; chemicals; coal; petroleum; paper and printing; food processing; textiles; and clothing. Agriculture is also a very important sector in the British economy. Its agriculture is highly mechanized and extremely productive; about 2% of the labor force produces 60% of the country's food needs. About one quarter of British land is arable with almost half suitable for meadows and pastures.

Greater London is considered the administrative and financial center and most important port. Liverpool is Britain's second port and is also part of the Merseyside conurbation along with Southport and Saint Helens. Greater Manchester has cotton and synthetic textiles, coal, and chemical industries and is a transportation and warehousing center. Leeds, Bradford, and the neighboring metropolitan districts are Britain's main center of woolen, worsted, and other textile production. Newcastle has coal mines and steel, electrical engineering, chemical, and shipbuilding and repair industries.

Swansea, Cardiff, and Newport are center of coal mining and steel manufacturing. Current important industries also include oil refining, metals production (lead, zinc, nickel, and aluminum), synthetic fibers, and electronics. In Scotland, the region around the River Clyde, including Glasgow, is noted for shipbuilding, marine engineering, and printing as well as textile, food, and chemicals production. The Belfast area in Northern Ireland is a shipbuilding, textile, and food products center.

2. China and UK Trade at 'Record High'

According to the latest economic statistics, the trade between China and the United Kingdom hit a 'record high' of £43bn in 2013, which also said that the UK's exports to China grew more than other EU countries.

The UK has been pushing to tap into China's domestic market. 'The UK can be the most profitable destination in the Western world for Chinese outward investment in infrastructure, real estate, energy and transportation. China and the UK working together will benefit our people and contribute to global peace and development', said Stephen Perry, chairman of the 48 Group Club, an independent business network that looks to promote ties between China and the UK Britain is among the top 10 nations globally for outbound Chinese investment and attracts more than double the investment of any other nation in Europe.

More and more Chinese firms are investing in the UK as they look to expand their global reach. Dalian Wanda Group has said it will spend £1bn to buy a British yacht maker and develop a hotel property in London. Network equipment maker Huawei has said it will invest £1.3bn in expanding its UK operations. Meanwhile, Beijing Construction Engineering Group (BCEG) will be part of a group investing £800m in Manchester Airport to develop its surrounding business.

案例 3 向南非 Thompson 公司出口手机

商业背景设定：

出口商：易联通迅设备公司（Yilian Communequip Co.,），中国最大的手机制造企业之一，产品畅销亚洲、欧美市场。目前公司正在大力拓展新兴市场客户，将南非设定为非洲市场业务的桥头堡，希望通过南非向整个非洲市场出口产品。

公司地址：中国广东省佛山市东广大街66号
销售总监：王庆
主要产品：智能手机

进口商：Thompson，南非最大家用电子产品进口商和销售商，在南非、津巴布韦、东非等国家拥有连锁品牌店，实力雄厚。
公司地址：459 Longhorns Dr., Cape Town
采购部经理：肖恩·霍尔（Shawn Hower）

易联通迅设备公司认为亚洲、欧美的智能手机市场已经接近饱和，手机生产厂商之间的竞争日趋激烈，产品利润下降明显，因此将非洲市场视为公司新的利润增长点。易联通迅进行了广泛的市场调查，发现价格在80美元左右的中低档智能手机正在迅速成为南非手机用户的热点，因此针对南非市场的需求，开发出一款价格在70美元的智能手机 ST - 511（Smart phone ST - 511）。易联通迅设备公司认为 Thompson 公司符合其业务拓展的需要，因此与 Thompson 公司取得联系，希望能和对方建立起良好的合作关系。

学习情境 1：建交函
(Correspondence for Establishing Business Relations)

知识目标： 1. 全面掌握建交函写作的要领。
2. 学习建交函写作的常用词组、典型句式。
3. 学习建交函写作的专业术语。
4. 学习建交函写作的商务背景知识。

能力目标： 1. 能够熟练运用本环节所学习的专业术语、常用词组、典型句式正确撰写建交函。
2. 掌握建交函写作所需要的相关商务背景知识。

任务：易联通迅设备公司销售总监王庆给 Thompson 公司采购部经理霍尔先生发出一封建交函，表达与对方合作的意愿，并且希望早日得到回复。

请就此撰写一封建交函。

要求如下：
1. 介绍本公司基本情况。
2. 表达合作意愿。

你可以借助资料库中的相关资料来撰写建交函。

范例：

Yilian Communequip Co.
No. 66 Dongguang Avenue,
Foshan, Guangdong

P. R. China
Jan. 20, 2015

Purchasing Department of Thompson
459 Longhorns Dr.
Cape Town, South Africa

Dear Mr. Hower,

We have obtained your name and address from the Commercial Counselor's Office of South African Embassy in Beijing, who informed us that you are the biggest importer of the domestic appliances in your country.

We produce the smart phones which have been very popular on the Asian, European and North American markets and our latest product ST – 511 is a phone especially developed for the South African market and is designed to meet the demands of the South African customers.

We hope this product will be of interest to you and enclosed please find our latest price list for your reference. Should you require any further details about our product, please do not hesitate to let us know.

We are looking forward to hearing from you soon.

Sincerely yours

Wang Qing

Chief Director of Sales

学习情境2：询盘函（Correspondence for Enquiry）

知识目标：1. 全面掌握询盘函写作的要领。
2. 学习询盘函的常用词组、典型句式。
3. 学习询盘函写作的专业术语。
4. 学习询盘函写作的商务背景知识。

能力目标：1. 能够熟练运用本环节所学习的专业术语、常用词组、典型句式正确撰写询盘函。
2. 掌握询盘函写作所需要的相关商务背景知识。

任务：Thompson公司非常重视易联通迅设备公司建立贸易关系的来函，认为与中国生产商的合作可以有效降低智能手机的购买成本，有助于公司进一步扩大市场占有率，巩固公司的地位，而易联通迅的 ST-511 手机的性能也非常适合南非市场的需求，因此决定和易联通迅设备公司进一步开展协商。霍尔先生回函王庆总监，感谢易联通迅的来信，表达合作意愿并请易联通迅设备公司能寄送样品以供深入的研究。

请就此撰写一封要求寄送样品的询盘函。
要求如下：
1. 感谢对方来电，表达合作的意向。
2. 要求寄送手机样品5部。

你可以借助资料库中的相关资料来撰写询盘函。

范例：

案例3 向南非 Thompson 公司出口手机

Jan. 30, 2015

Dear Mr. Wang,

Your letter of Jan. 20 has been received with great pleasure and we are presently keen to find a trustworthy Chinese partner.

The quality and technological features of your product are very impressive and we hope that you could send us 5 phones for further tests.

We are looking forward to your favorable reply.

Sincerely yours

Shawn Hower

President

任务： Thompson 公司很快就收到了易联通迅设备公司寄来的智能手机样品，相关测试证明这款产品完全符合南非政府相关法规的要求，并且获得了较高的客户满意度，因此决定与易联通迅设备公司开展业务。霍尔先生致函王庆总监，告知对方计划订购 ST-511 型智能手机 5000 部，要求易联通迅设备公司进行报价。

请就此撰写一封要求报价的询盘函。

要求如下：

1. 对寄送样品表示满意，表示要订购 5000 部手机。
2. 请求易联通迅设备公司对此进行报价。

你可以借助资料库中的相关资料来撰写询盘函。

范例：

Feb. 20, 2015

Dear Mr. Wang,

We are pleased to tell you that your samples have been tested and the results are very successful. We are sure this product will be very popular with our customers and we would like to ask you quote us the lowest FOB Zhanjiang for 5000 phones, stating your earliest delivery date, term of payment and discount for regular purchases.

If your price is reasonable, you can expect larger orders from us.

We are awaiting your early replies.

Sincerely yours

Shawn Hower

学习情境3：发盘函（Correspondence for Offers）

知识目标：1. 全面掌握发盘函写作的要领。
　　　　　2. 学习发盘函写作的常用词组、典型句式。
　　　　　3. 学习发盘函写作的专业术语。
　　　　　4. 学习发盘函写作的商务背景知识。
能力目标：1. 能够熟练运用本环节所学习的专业术语、常用词组、典型句式正确撰写发盘函。
　　　　　2. 掌握发盘函写作所需要的相关商务背景知识。

任务：易联通迅设备公司收到霍尔先生的询盘函后，判断Thomson的确有诚意与公司开展业务往来，决定抓住这个机会，因此迅速向其发盘。
请就此撰写一封发盘函。
要求如下：
品名：ST-511自动智能手机
颜色：黑色
单价：每部70美元，FOB湛江
折扣：5%
数量：5000部
包装：牛皮纸箱，每箱100部
交货期：收到信用证后4周内发货

保险：由买方投保

支付方式：保兑的、不可撤销见票即付信用证

发盘有效期为3周

你可以借助资料库中的相关资料来撰写发盘函。

范例：

Mar. 10, 2015

Dear Mr. Hower,

Your enquiry dated Feb. 20 has been received and we are very happy to start business with you. Our offers are as follows.

    Commodity：ST-511Smart phone
    Color：black
    Price：US＄70, FOB Zhanjiang
    Discount rate：5%
    Quantity：5000
    Packing：100 in a craft paper box
    Delivery：within 4 weeks of receiving L/C
    Insurance：to be covered by the buyer
    Term of Payment：by confirmed, irrevocable L/C at sight

We believe this price would be very competitive at your market. Our offer will be revoked if not accepted within 3 weeks.

Your early decision would be appreciated.

Yours faithfully

Wang Qing

识别虚假询盘的小诀窍

外贸业务员每天都会收到很多询盘，但是其中有很多是无用或者虚假的询盘。如果你发了详细的资料或者报价，有可能泄漏自己的信息，所以识别真假客户非常重要。那么如何有效识别虚假询盘呢？

第一，查发件人的 IP。这项工作可以通过一些专业的 IP 查询网站进行。方法：右键单击收到的邮件，选择属性—详细信息，在里面会看到 IP 地址，再到类似于 http：//www.ip138.com 之类的网站里，把 IP 复制上去就可以查到了。

第二，如果公司网站有计数器，同时可以参考一下计数器里面的 IP 记录，看看是不是有这个 IP 浏览过公司网站。用计数器还可以知道浏览网页的人是如何找到你的，是点击 B2B 网站上面的链接还是直接输入网站地址。如果是直接输入地址，那就要想想他是怎么知道的。

第三，看看客户发来邮件的时间，根据时差判断客户发送邮件的时间，比如早上八九点收到了从美国 IP 发送过来的邮件，这时就要打个问号了。

第四，看客户在邮件里面是否留了详细的联系资料。可信度较高的客户会留下网址、详细电话、传真、地址等。对于资料不全的，可以询问其联系方式。感觉有问题的，可以发送传真或者电话询问一下。打电话给客户会让客户觉得你比较重视他。

第五，分析客户询盘的内容。如果有具体的规格、详细的要求，这类客户比较有价值。如果只是笼统的要样本、价格单什么的，则没有实际意义。

学习情境4：还盘函（Correspondence for Counter-offers）

知识目标：1. 全面掌握还盘函写作的要领。
　　　　　　2. 学习还盘函写作的常用词组、典型句式。
　　　　　　3. 学习还盘函写作的专业术语。
　　　　　　4. 学习还盘函写作的商务背景知识。

能力目标：1. 能够熟练运用本环节所学习的专业术语、常用词组、典型句式正确撰写还盘函。
　　　　　　2. 掌握还盘函写作所需要的相关商务背景知识。

任务：Thompson 收到易联通迅设备公司的报价后，认为当前南非消费者普遍消费能力不强，这个价格偏高，不利于未来的销售和公司盈利，因此致函王庆总监，希望能得到更加优惠的价格。

请就此撰写一封还盘函。

要求如下：

1. 告知易联通迅设备公司报价偏高。
2. 说明这一价格在市场上无法赢得竞争。
3. 希望单价能够降到 50 美元。

你可以借助资料库中的相关资料来撰写还盘函。

范例:

Mar. 21, 2015

Dear Mr. Wang,

We are obliged for your letter of Mar. 10 quoting for ST-511 smart phones at $70 each one, but regret to inform you we cannot place an order at this price considering the consumption capacity of our customers. We therefore hope you can lower your price to $50 each. If you cannot do so, we have to regretfully decline your offer.

We are anticipating your favorable reply.

Yours faithfully

Shawn Hower

Thompson

任务： 易联通迅设备公司对于Thompson的还盘函进行了研究，认为50美元的还价已经超过了公司的承受能力。综合各种情况，经过认真测算后，公司决定将60美元设定为最低单价。
请就此撰写一封还盘函。
要求如下：
1. 对Thompson公司未能接受己方的报价表示遗憾。
2. 表示已经有南非进口商和本公司取得联系。
3. 表示为了今后的合作，同意将价格降至60美元，此报价为最终价格。

你可以借助资料库中的相关资料来撰写还盘函。

范例:

Mar. 30, 2015

Dear Mr. Hower,

Thank you for your letter and we are disappointed that our price has been rejected. Honestly speaking, this offer is quite realistic and we have get contacted with several dealers in your country who tend to consider our price reasonable.

Considering the future friendly business relations, we can offer you the most favorable price of $60 each. We must point out that this price is the final offer.

Yours faithfully

Wang Qing

学习情境5：订单函（Correspondence for Orders）

知识目标： 1. 全面掌握订单函写作的要领。
2. 学习订单函写作的常用词组、典型句式。
3. 学习订单函写作的专业术语。
4. 学习订单函写作的商务背景知识。

能力目标： 1. 能够熟练运用本环节所学习的专业术语、常用词组、典型句式正确撰写订单函。
2. 掌握订单函写作所需要的相关商务背景知识。

任务： 收到易联通迅设备公司的最新报价后，Thompson经过研究，认为这一价格虽然高于公司预期，但是综合考虑其性价比，和市场上类似的产品相比较仍然具有比较突出的竞争优势，因此愿意接受易联通迅设备公司的报价，决定首批订购5000部手机。
请就此撰写一封订单函。
要求如下：
1. 订购5000部黑色ST-511智能手机
2. 每部60美元，FOB湛江
3. 牛皮纸箱，每箱100部
4. 收到信用证后4周内发货

5. 保险由买方投保
6. 支付方式为不可撤销的即期信用证

你可以借助资料库中的相关资料来撰写订单函。

范例：

April 10, 2015

Dear Mr. Wang,

We hereby inform you that after considering your offers we finally decide to place an initial order with you for the following.

  Commodity: ST-511 Smart Phone
  Color: black
  Quantity: 5000
  Price: US $60 each, FOB Zhanjiang
  Packing: 100 sets in a craft paper box
  Delivery: within 4 weeks of receiving L/C
  Insurance: to be covered by the buyer
  Term of Payment: by irrevocable L/C at sight

Please make sure the quality of the merchandise is in strict accordance with the samples and we believe the success of this initial order will lead to bigger deals between us.

Sincerely yours

Shawn Hower

Thompson

学习情境6：支付方式函（Correspondence for Terms of Payment）

知识目标：1. 全面掌握支付方式函写作的要领。

2. 学习支付方式函写作的常用词组、典型句式。
3. 学习支付方式函写作的专业术语。
4. 学习支付方式函写作的商务背景知识。

能力目标：1. 能够熟练运用本环节所学习的专业术语、常用词组、典型句式正确撰写支付方式函。
2. 掌握支付方式函写作所需要的相关商务背景知识。

任务：根据前期的商谈结果，Thompson 和易联通迅设备公司签署了编号为 YTI – 13960 号的销售合同。Thompson 按照合同要求按期在银行开立了信用证，并迅速通知了易联通迅设备公司。

请就此撰写一封开立信用证通知函。

要求如下：

1. 通知易联通迅设备公司根据双方签订的编号为 FFI – 1354 的合同，Thompson 已经在南非第一国民银行开立了编号为 35421 的以易联通迅设备公司为受益人的不可撤销的跟单信用证。
2. 金额为 300000 美元。
3. 信用证有效期为 2015 年 10 月 20 日。

你可以借助资料库中的相关资料来撰写开立信用证通知函。

范例：

April 25, 2015

Dear Mr. Wang Qing,

RE: L/C for 5000 ST – 511 Smartphones

We are happy to inform you that we have instructed the First National Bank of South Africa to open an irrevocable documentary letter of credit No. 35421 in your favor. The amount is US $ 300000 and is valid until 20th October, 2015. The L/C will be sent to you very soon.

Yours faithfully

Shawn Hower

任务： 易联通迅设备公司根据合同的要求开始了手机的生产制造，但是由于面板制造工厂发生事故，零件供应出现暂时的短缺，导致易联通迅无法在原定的时间发货，因此希望对信用证进行展期，将原定的发货日期推迟到 8 月 31 日。

请就此撰写一封信用证展期的请求函。

要求如下：
1. 说明请求信用证展期的原因。
2. 希望将发货日期更改为 8 月 31 日。

你可以借助资料库中的相关资料来撰写更改支付方式请求函。

范例：

May 10, 2015

Dear Mr. Hower,

Thank you for your establishment of the L/C, but we are very sorry to tell you that a fire accident took place in our phone screen plant. And although we have tried our best to find a new supplier, we are afraid that a delay on the delivery will be unavoidable. Therefore, we would appreciate it if you would kindly agree to extend the delivery date of your L/C to August 31.

We are grateful if you could kindly consider this request.

Sincerely yours

Wang Qing

谨防信用证圈套

赵先生经朋友介绍与某国中间商 A 先生谈成了价值 100 万美金的电机出口项目。A 在信用证开出之前提出把实际货款提高 20% 作为佣金，并且要求赵先生提前支付此佣金款。赵先生提出在自己的开户行确认信用证后马上支付。外商很快在一家国外银行开出了信用证，赵先生在银行确认后支付了 20% 的佣金。外商收到佣金后以种种理由使得生意最终没有做成，赵先生准备索赔时才发现信用证有一项软条款：买方验货签字。此刻赵先生这才明白自己受骗了，而且由于已经安排了材料采购和商品生产，公司蒙受了巨大的损失。

骗子之所以能够得逞，关键原因就是赵先生不熟悉信用证的操作及其特性，没有认真审核信用证，并且在没有收回货款之前就贸然付款给买方，而骗子正是利用以信用证"买方验货签字"的软条款，致使赵先生方因为拿不到买方验货签字的文件而无法保证单证相符回收货款。

当卖方遇到中间商加价后要求返回差价款时，合理的规范操作应该是在收回全部货款后再予兑现。如果买方在未实际履行合同或在支付全部货款前就要求卖方提前支付差价、回扣，一定要提高警惕，必须以收妥全部货款后再兑现为交易的底线。

学习情境 7：包装函（Correspondence for Packing）

知识目标： 1. 全面掌握包装函写作的要领。
2. 学习包装函写作的常用词组、典型句式。
3. 学习包装函写作的专业术语。
4. 学习包装函写作的商务背景知识。

能力目标： 1. 能够熟练运用本环节所学习的专业术语、常用词组、典型句式正确撰写包装函。
2. 掌握包装函写作所需要的相关商务背景知识。

任务： Thompson 公司发现合同中关于包装的条款不是非常明确清晰，因此致信易联通迅设备公司，再次明确包装相关的条款和包装要求，强调务必按照要求对产品进行认真的包装。

请就此撰写一封包装指示函。

要求如下：
1. 强调包装必须符合长途海运的要求。
2. 要求将手机用防水纸包裹后放置在木箱中，每 100 部手机一箱。
3. 强调防潮、防震。

你可以借助资料库中的相关资料来撰写包装指示函。

范例：

Jun. 20, 2015

Dear Mr. Wang,

After going through the contract, we find that the packing clause is not clear enough and we have to reiterate that the relative clause should read as follows.

Packing: seaworthy packing suitable for long distance marine transportation.

To eliminate any future trouble, we shall make clear the packing requirements as follows.

The mobile phones should be wrapped with waterproof paper before being placed in the wooden case and every wooden case should contain no more than 100 phones.

The goods must be well protected against moisture and shock.

We look forward to hearing from you.

Yours sincerely

Shawn Hower

学习情境 8：保险函（Correspondence for Insurance）

知识目标：1. 全面掌握保险函写作的要领。
2. 学习保险函写作的常用词组、典型句式。
3. 学习保险函写作的专业术语。
4. 学习保险函写作的商务背景知识。

能力目标：1. 能够熟练运用本环节所学习的专业术语、常用词组、典型句式正确撰写保险函。
2. 掌握保险函写作所需要的相关商务背景知识。

任务：经过多方努力后，易联通迅设备公司终于完成了手机的生产任务，致信 Thompson，要求其为相关商品购买保险。但是 Thompson 希望易联通迅能够代为投保。

请就此撰写一封要求卖方代为购买保险的请求函。

要求如下：

1. 请求易联通迅按发票金额的110%代为购买一切险。
2. 承诺收到账单后会立即付还易联通迅所垫付的保费。

你可以借助资料库中的相关资料来撰写保险函。

范例：

July 10, 2015

Dear Mr. Wang,

RE: Insurance Covering S/C No. YTI-13960 for 5000 ST-511 Smartphones.

We are so glad that the production of the Smartphones has been successfully completed and do appreciate your efforts. As we desire to have the goods insured at your end, would you please insure the consignment on our behalf against All Risks for 110% of the invoice value. We shall refund the premium immediately upon receipt of your debit note.

Your approval would be highly appreciated and if you have any further instructions, please do not hesitate to contact us.

Yours sincerely

Hower

学习情境9：运输函（Correspondence for Shipment）

知识目标：1. 全面掌握运输函写作的要领。
2. 学习运输函写作的常用词组、典型句式。
3. 学习运输函写作的专业术语。
4. 学习运输函写作的商务背景知识。

能力目标：1. 能够熟练运用本环节所学习的专业术语、常用词组、典型句式正确撰写运输函。

案例3　向南非Thompson公司出口手机

2. 掌握运输函写作所需要的相关商务背景知识。

任务：Thompson 按照合同规定，在货轮 Greatania 上预订了仓位。近期收到了轮船公司通知，Greatania 将在 9 月 10 日左右从湛江港起航。Thomson 公司给易联通讯发出了通知。
请就此撰写一封告知对方起运时间的通知函。
要求如下：
1. 告知对方起运时间。
2. 要求对方尽快完成装运工作。

你可以借助资料库中的相关资料来撰写通知函。

范例：

July 20, 2015

Dear Mr. Wang Qing,

We have been informed by the shipping company that S/S Greatania is due to sail from Zhanjiang Port on or about September 10, on which we have booked room for the smartphones.

We would like you to arrange shipment of the goods with least possible delay.

Your close cooperation in this respect will be highly appreciated.

Sincerely yours

Shawn Hower

学习情境 10：索赔和纠纷解决
(Correspondence for Claim and Settlement)

知识目标：1. 全面掌握索赔函写作的要领。
2. 学习索赔函写作的常用词组、典型句式。

3. 学习索赔函写作的专业术语。
4. 学习索赔函写作的商务背景知识。

能力目标： 1. 能够熟练运用本环节所学习的专业术语、常用词组、典型句式正确撰写索赔函。
2. 掌握索赔函写作所需要的相关商务背景知识。

任务： 经过两个多月的长途海运后，Thomson 公司订购的手机终于顺利抵达德班港。但是很遗憾的是 Thompson 验收货物时，发现有一个木箱内的手机并非合同中规定的 ST－511 型智能手机，因此提出索赔。

请就此撰写一封索赔函。

要求如下：
1. 告知易联通迅设备公司货物已收到。
2. 告知对方有一箱手机并非订购的型号，因此要求赔偿 1 万美元。

你可以借助资料库中的相关资料来撰写索赔函。

范例：

Oct. 10, 2015

Dear Mr. Wang Qing,

We have received the ordered goods, but we were surprised and disappointed to find after careful examination that the phones in one wooden case are not ST－511 as stipulated in our sales contract.

Needless to say, this will affect our sales seriously as we have received the orders from our customers for ST－511 phones. We, therefore, have to ask you US $ 10000 for compensation.

We are looking forward to a satisfactory conclusion of this problem.

Yours respectfully

案例3　向南非 Thompson 公司出口手机

Shawn Hower

任务：经过公司紧急调查，易联通迅设备公司发现的确是由于自己的失误，造成错发了一箱手机，因此致函 Thompson，告知其调查结果和公司的解决方案。

请就此撰写一封索赔回复函。

要求如下：

1. 告知 Thompson，经过公司调查，的确有一箱手机型号与合同不符。

2. 公司对此提出两个解决方案：立刻将 100 部手机通过空运直接送往开普敦，或者提供 7000 美元的特别折扣。

你可以借助资料库中的相关资料来撰写索赔回复函。

范例：

Oct. 25, 2015

Dear Mr. Hower,

RE: Inconsistency of 100 Smartphones

After serious internal investigation, we found with great regret that one wooden box containing 100 SM-511 smartphones was transported to you by mistake. We sincerely apologize for this carelessness.

To solve the problem, we would like either send the correct type of smartphones by air freight directly to Cape Town on our expense or pay you 7000 as special allowance.

Please accept our sincere apology and we look forward to your decision as to which is preferable to you.

Sincerely yours

Wang Qing

商业背景知识拓展

1. Introduction of South Africa Economy

Being one of the biggest and most stable economies in Africa, South Africa is a middle-income country, with fully developed basic infrastructure. The manufacturing, mining and service sectors are the largest contributors to the country's GDP. Cape Town, Port Elizabeth, Durban and Johannesburg are the primary source of trade for the South African economy.

South Africa has abundant natural resources, well developed regulatory systems and an established manufacturing base. The country's modern infrastructure supports the efficient distribution of goods throughout the southern African region. The economy has a marked duality, with a sophisticated financial and industrial economy having grown alongside an underdeveloped informal economy. It is this second economy which presents both potential and a developmental challenge.

Over the past decade, substantial increases in government social service spending have helped reduce poverty, but now the government has begun to place a greater emphasis on infrastructure, employment and economic growth. Money will be spent on improving the energy sector to double electricity generation, on transport and logistics, hospitals and clinics, and on education infrastructure as an investment in human capital.

One of the most important elements of South Arica's New Growth Plan is a green economy, and the potential the creation of a lower-carbon economy has as a potential job generator as well as a spur for industrial development. In 2011, the government entered into the Green Economic Accord, which aims to create 300000 jobs in the next 10 years through investment in the green economy. In 2012, the Treasury allocated R800-million over two years to the Green Fund, which aims to provide finance for high-quality, high-impact, job-creating green economy projects around the country.

2. Bilateral Trade with China on the Increase

South Africa's bilateral trade with China has increased sharply for several years, but the composition of the trade was a matter of concern as South Africa's exports comprised mainly of raw materials. Over 90% of South Africa's top 10 exports to China are in raw materials while 100% of its top 10 imports from China are manufactured products. The South African and Chinese governments have recognized that this structure of trade is not sustainable and have agreed to work together to correct the situation.

Many believe that there is scope to expand South Africa's exports to China in value-added manufactured products, particularly as the Chinese economy continued to register strong growth rates. Also, China is in the process of re-orientating its economic development strategy away from reliance on exports and inward investment to one based more on domestic consumption and the development of its interior regions.

The South Africa government tries to promote the export of value-added manufactured products to China, mainly by means of trade exhibitions. The investments from China are growing, but off a low base, which has been spread across the metals, car, communications, financial service, food and tobacco, chemicals, industrial machinery, construction, engines and turbines, and transportation sectors. The China-Africa Development Fund has also reported that there are joint investment projects, particularly in the mining, financial, appliances and information and communications technology sectors. Both sides have agreed to work towards a more equitable trade balance, and a joint working group on trade statistics was established under the binational commission to address the trade imbalance.

案例 4　向俄罗斯 Zukov 公司出口苹果

商业背景设定：

出口商：山东鲁农农业公司（Shandong Lunong Agriculture Co.,），中国农业生产龙头企业，公司生产和销售包括水果、谷物、蔬菜、水产品在内的多种农产品，其生产的富士苹果、鸭梨、水蜜桃等水果畅销日本、韩国、欧美等地。近年来随着中俄贸易往来的逐步增多，对俄农产品出口业务也迅速提升。鲁农公司也调整了出口布局，将俄罗斯设定为公司未来发展的战略市场。

公司地址：中国山东省烟台市栖霞街 366 号
总经理：刘强
主要产品：优质有机红富士苹果

进口商：Zukov，俄罗斯最大的连锁超市集团之一，在莫斯科、圣彼得堡等大城市开设了上百家大中型超市，年营业额达到 100 多亿美元。

公司地址：3329 Puhitinvo Boulevard.，Moscow
总经理：尤里·巴尔舍夫（Yuri Barsherv）

由于日本、韩国、美国、德国等国家开始实施更多的农业保护措施，并且利用绿色壁垒等多种手段限制国外农产品的进口，鲁农公司在其传统市场上的利润空间出现了明显的下降。鲁农公司针对这些变化开始调整市场布局，决定大力开拓新兴市场国家。俄罗斯重工业发达，但是由于气候等原因，农业生产相对滞后，尤其是水果品种较少，价格较高。鲁农将其定位为公司新的利润增长点。

鲁农公司经过长期市场调查，认为 Zukov 公司实力雄厚，有完善的营销网络和较高知名度，非常符合其业务拓展的需要，因此希望能与 Zukov 公司建立合作关系。

学习情境 1：建交函
(Correspondence for Establishing Business Relations)

知识目标： 1. 全面掌握建交函写作的要领。
　　　　　　 2. 学习建交函写作的常用词组、典型句式。
　　　　　　 3. 学习建交函写作的专业术语。

4. 学习建交函写作的商务背景知识。

能力目标： 1. 能够熟练运用本环节所学习的专业术语、常用词组、典型句式正确撰写建交函。

2. 掌握建交函写作所需要的相关商务背景知识。

任务： 鲁农公司总经理刘强给 Zukov 公司总经理 Barsherv 先生发出一封建交函，表达与对方合作的意愿，并且希望早日得到回复。

请就此撰写一封建交函。

要求如下：

1. 介绍本公司基本情况。
2. 表达合作意愿。

你可以借助资料库中的相关资料来撰写建交函。

范例：

Lunong Agriculture Co.
No. 366 Qixia Street,
Yantai, Shandong
P. R. China
Jan. 20, 2015

Zukov
3329 Puhitinvo Boulevard.,
Moscow, Russia

Dear Mr. Barsherv,

We learn your name and address from Robin & Rousse Ltd in England and understand you are the biggest supermarket franchiser in Russia. We are informed that you are big buyer of Chinese agricultural product, which comes within our line of business. As one of the leading agricultural enterprises in China, our products are very popular on the Japanese, Korean, European and American markets and we hope the business and friendship can be promoted by our joint efforts.

To acquaint you with our products, we enclose a copy of our major agricultural products which are available for Russian market at present and we believe they will be of interest to you.

Should you require any further details about our products, please do not hesitate to let us know.

We are looking forward to hearing from you soon.

Sincerely yours

Liu Qiang

General Manager

学习情境2：询盘函（Correspondence for Enquiry）

知识目标：1. 全面掌握询盘函写作的要领。
2. 学习询盘函的常用词组、典型句式。
3. 学习询盘函写作的专业术语。
4. 学习询盘函写作的商务背景知识。

能力目标：1. 能够熟练运用本环节所学习的专业术语、常用词组、典型句式正确撰写询盘函。
2. 掌握询盘函写作所需要的相关商务背景知识。

任务：Zukov 公司正在努力建立来自中国的、可靠的农产品供应渠道，因此非常重视鲁农公司建立贸易关系的来函。Zukov 公司经过研究，认为这家公司农产品品种丰富、产量较大、质优价廉，非常适合俄罗斯消费者的需求，与之开展合作可以保障持续稳定的货物供应，并且降低购买成本，因此决定和鲁农公司进行贸易联系。Barsherv 先生回函刘强总经理，感谢鲁农公司的来信，表达合作意愿并请鲁农公司寄送样品。

请就此撰写一封要求寄送样品的询盘函。

要求如下：
1. 感谢对方来电，表明公司希望双方能够紧密合作。
2. 要求寄送有机苹果和苹果干样品。

你可以借助资料库中的相关资料来撰写询盘函。

范例：

Jan. 30, 2015

Dear Mr. Liu,

Thank you for your letter of Jan. 20 and we shall be very glad to enter business with you.

We are impressed by the variety and quality of your products and suppose they will be welcomed by our customers. Therefore, we should be grateful if you could send us some samples of your organic apple and dried apple chips.

We are looking forward to your prompt reply.

Sincerely yours

Yuri Barsherv

President

任务：鲁农公司收到 Zukov 公司的回复函后，精心挑选了所要求的样品并迅速寄送出去。Zukov 公司收到鲁农公司寄来的苹果和苹果干样品后，经过检验证明这些产品完全符合俄罗斯关于农产品进口质量的要求，其品质超越了公司现有供应商的产品，决定与鲁农公司开展进口业务。Barsherv 先生致函刘强总经理，告知对方计划订购有机苹果 5 吨，有机苹果干 1000 盒，要求鲁农公司对该批货物报价。

请就此撰写一封要求报价的询盘函。

要求如下：
1. 对寄送样品表示满意，表示要订购有机苹果 5 吨，有机苹果干 1000 盒。
2. 请求鲁农公司报 FOB 青岛价。

你可以借助资料库中的相关资料来撰写询盘函。

范例:

Feb. 20, 2015

Dear Mr. Liu,

Your samples have been received with many thanks and we are very satisfied with the quality of your products and hope our customers will like them too.

Please let us know your lowest possible price for the relevant goods and we would rather you quote us FOB Qing dao for 5 tons of organic apple and 1000 boxes of dried apple chips.

If your price is competitive, we can place order right away.

We are awaiting your early replies.

Sincerely yours

Yuri Barsherv

外贸付款欺诈案例辨析

　　某中国贸易公司向美国 X 公司出口玩具，付款方式为即期 L/C。X 公司随后要求寄送 1/3 正本 B/L 以便早日提货销售，并一再声称这是美国商界的通行做法。因是与对方的第一次交易，中国公司拒绝了此要求。X 公司则坚持不寄不成交。最后在 X 公司签署保函，保证即使没有收到 1/3 提单时也按时依据 L/C 要求付款后，双方签署合同。第一次合作很顺利，在中国公司刚刚寄出 B/L 后不久就收到了 L/C 项下的付款。第二次交易时 X 公司仍坚持带 1/3 正本 B/L。考虑到客户第一单很守信用并及时付款，中国公司答应了客户要求。货发出后，就及时将正本 B/L 寄出并迅速向银行交单议付。十几天后，中国公司询问 X 公司是否已经付款时，客户回复说正在办理。二十几天后中国公司发现货款仍未到账，追问 X 公司是否已付款。对方称因资金紧张，需要推迟几日付款。实际上此时 X 公司已凭寄去的正本 B/L 将货提走。三十几天后当中国公司再次要求 X 公司付款时，对方开始拖延，后来就彻底失去联系，中国公司白白损失数十万元。

学习情境 3：发盘函（Correspondence for Offers）

知识目标： 1. 全面掌握发盘函写作的要领。
2. 学习发盘函写作的常用词组、典型句式。
3. 学习发盘函写作的专业术语。
4. 学习发盘函写作的商务背景知识。

能力目标： 1. 能够熟练运用本环节所学习的专业术语、常用词组、典型句式正确撰写发盘函。
2. 掌握发盘函写作所需要的相关商务背景知识。

任务： 鲁农公司收到 Zukov 公司的询盘函后，经过认真的测算，向 Zukov 公司发出了详细的实盘。

请就此撰写一封发盘函。

要求如下：

品名：有机苹果和苹果干

价格：FOB 青岛价，苹果每吨 800 美元，苹果干每盒 10 美元

数量：有机苹果 5 吨，苹果干 1000 盒

包装：苹果 100 千克装 1 木箱，10 箱装一个集装箱，苹果干 24 盒装一货盘，100 货盘装一个集装箱

交货期：收到信用证后 4 周内发货

保险：由卖方投保

支付方式：保兑的、不可撤销见票即付信用证

发盘有效期为 4 周

你可以借助资料库中的相关资料来撰写发盘函。

范例：

Mar. 10, 2015

Dear Mr. Barsherv,

Replying your enquiry of Feb. 10 for our organic apple and dried apple chips, we are pleased to quote as follows.

 Commodity: Organic apple and dried apple chips
 Price: Apple: US $ 800 per ton,
     Dried apple chips: US $ 10 per box
     FOB Qingdao
 Quantity: 5 tons of apple and 1000 boxes of dried apple chips
 Packing: Apple: Every 100 kg in a wooden case, 100 cases in a FCL container
     Dried apple chips: Every 24 boxes on a pallet, 10 pallets in a FCL container
 Delivery: within 4 weeks of receiving L/C
 Insurance: to be covered by the seller
 Term of Payment: by confirmed, irrevocable L/C at sight

We believe this price is very competitive at your market and the offer is valid for 4 weeks.

We are looking forward to your early and favorable decision.

Yours faithfully

Liu Qiang

学习情境4：还盘函（Correspondence for Counter-offers）

  知识目标：1. 全面掌握还盘函写作的要领。
      2. 学习还盘函写作的常用词组、典型句式。
      3. 学习还盘函写作的专业术语。
      4. 学习还盘函写作的商务背景知识。
  能力目标：1. 能够熟练运用本环节所学习的专业术语、常用词组、典型句式正确撰写还盘函。
      2. 掌握还盘函写作所需要的相关商务背景知识。

  任务：Zukov 收到鲁农公司的报价后，认为由于俄罗斯目前经济状况不佳，消费者的消费意愿和能力均呈现下降趋势，因此认为鲁农的报价偏高，于是致函刘强总经理，希望鲁农公司降低价格。

  请就此撰写一封还盘函。
  要求如下：
1. 告知鲁农公司报价偏高。
2. 希望苹果的价格降到 700 美元/吨，苹果干的价格降到 5 美元/盒。

你可以借助资料库中的相关资料来撰写还盘函。

范例：

Mar. 21, 2015

Dear Mr. Liu,

Your letter of Mar. 10 quoting for organic apple and dried apple chips has been received with many thanks.

Although your products are good in quality, we regret to inform you that we cannot place an order at this price because of the latest economic crises which has considerably hampered the consumption intention and capacity of our clients. To enter into the business, we suggest that you could lower your price to US $700/ton for apple and US $5/box for apple chips. We believe this pricing is realistic and mutually beneficial in the long run.

Your favorable reply is anticipated.

Yours faithfully

Yuri Barsherv

Zukov

  任务：鲁农公司对于 Zukov 的还盘函进行了研究，认为苹果 700 美元/吨的还价可以接受，但是苹果干 5 美元/盒的价格是公司无法承受的。因此经过多次的认真测算后，公司决定接受 Zukov 公司对于苹果的还价，但是拒绝对方对于苹果干的还价。

请就此撰写一封还盘函。

要求如下：

1. 对 Zukov 公司未能接受己方的报价表示遗憾。

2. 说明为了今后的合作，同意将苹果的价格降至 700 美元/吨，但是无法接受对于苹果干的还价。

3. 告知对方此价格为最终报价。

你可以借助资料库中的相关资料来撰写还盘函。

范例：

Mar. 30, 2015

Dear Mr. Barsherv,

We are disappointed that you rejected our offer, which we consider a reasonable price. In view of the future business relations and successful cooperation, we have decided to lower the price of apple to 700 dollars per ton, but the demand for lower price for dried apply chips cannot be satisfied.

We must point out that this offer is final and your prompt reply would be highly appreciated.

Yours faithfully

Liu Qiang

学习情境 5：订单函 (Correspondence for Orders)

知识目标：1. 全面掌握订单函写作的要领。

2. 学习订单函写作的常用词组、典型句式。

3. 学习订单函写作的专业术语。

4. 学习订单函写作的商务背景知识。

能力目标：1. 能够熟练运用本环节所学习的专业术语、常用词组、典型句式正确撰写订单函。
2. 掌握订单函写作所需要的相关商务背景知识。

任务：收到鲁农公司的最新报价后，Zukov认为虽然对方拒绝了对于苹果干的还价，但是苹果报价的降低对于公司更为有利，而且综合考虑其性价比，总体而言，这个报价还是令人满意的，因此愿意接受鲁农公司的报价，决定下订单。

请就此撰写一封订单函。

要求如下：

品名：有机苹果和苹果干

价格：FOB青岛，苹果每吨700美元，苹果干每盒10美元

数量：有机苹果5吨，苹果干1000盒

包装：苹果100千克装1木箱，10箱装一个集装箱；苹果干10盒装一货盘，100货盘装一个集装箱

交货期：收到信用证后4周内发货

保险：由卖方投保

支付方式：保兑的、不可撤销见票即付信用证

你可以借助资料库中的相关资料来撰写订单函。

范例：

April 10, 2015

Dear Mr. Liu,

We are pleased in sending you the order confirmation covering our purchase from you of organic apple and dried apple chips and the order is as follows.

 Commodity：Organic apple and dried apple chips
 Price：Apple：US $ 700 per ton,
   Dried apple chips：US $ 10 per box
   FOB Qingdao
 Quantity：5 tons of apple and 1000 boxes of dried apple chips

Packing: Apple: Every 100 kg in a wooden case, 10 cases in a FCL container
Dried apple chips: Every 10 boxes on a pallet, 100 pallets in a FCL container
Delivery: within 4 weeks of receiving L/C
Insurance: to be covered by the seller
Term of Payment: by confirmed, irrevocable L/C at sight

If the quality of your initial consignment turns out satisfactory, we assure you that regular orders will follow.

Sincerely yours

Zukov

学习情境 6：支付方式函（Correspondence for Term of Payment）

知识目标：1. 全面掌握支付方式函写作的要领。
2. 学习支付方式函写作的常用词组、典型句式。
3. 学习支付方式函写作的专业术语。
4. 学习支付方式函写作的商务背景知识。

能力目标：1. 能够熟练运用本环节所学习的专业术语、常用词组、典型句式正确撰写支付方式函。
2. 掌握支付方式函写作所需要的相关商务背景知识。

任务：Zukov 按照与鲁农公司签署的编号为 TYI-60139 号销售合同在银行开立信用证，并通知鲁农公司。

请就此撰写一封开立信用证通知函。

要求如下：

1. 通知鲁农公司根据双方签订的编号为 TYI-60139 的合同，Zukov 已经在俄罗斯国家银行开立了保兑的不可撤销的即期信用证，受益人为鲁农公司，编号是 21489。
2. 信用证金额为 13500 美元。
3. 信用证有效期为 2015 年 10 月 20 日。

你可以借助资料库中的相关资料来撰写开立信用证通知函。

范例：

案例 4　向俄罗斯 Zukov 公司出口苹果

April 25, 2015

Dear Mr. Liu Qiang,

RE: L/C for Organic Apple and Dried Apple Chips

We have instructed the National Bank of Russia Federation to open a confirmed, irrevocable letter of credit for US $13500 in your favor, valid until 20 October. The number of the L/C is 21489.

The L/C will be sent to you very soon.

Yours faithfully

Yuri Barsherv

任务： 鲁农公司很快收到了 Zukov 公司寄送的信用证，但是审证后发现信用证与销售合同的条款有不符之处，因此致函 Zukov 公司要求其进行修改。

请就此撰写一封信用证修改的通知函。

要求如下：

1. 说明信用证与合同有不符之处。
2. 要求将报价由 FOB Hamburg 改为 FOB Qingdao。
3. 指出信用证应为保兑的、不可撤销信用证，而非仅仅是不可撤销信用证。

你可以借助资料库中的相关资料来撰写更改支付方式请求函。

范例：

May 10, 2015

Dear Mr. Barsherv,

Thank you for your L/C No. 21489, but we are very sorry to tell you that we have found tow discrepancies. "FOB Hamburg" should be "FOB Qingdao" and the L/C should be "confirmed and irrevocable" instead of "irrevocable".

We are grateful if you could kindly make the amendments a. s. a. p.

Sincerely yours

Liu Qiang

常用付款方式的风险分析

D/A (document against acceptance): 承兑交单。它是在跟单托收方式下,出口方(或代收银行)向进口方以承兑为条件交付单据的一种办法,即汇票付款人(进口方)在代收银行提示远期汇票时,对汇票的认可行为。这种支付方式的风险较大。银行收到出口商的单据后,要求进口商签字承诺到期付款,然后会将单据转交给进口商。如果进口商拒绝付款,银行不承担任何责任,出口方会面临货款、货物两空的后果。

学习情境7:包装函(Correspondence for Packing)

知识目标: 1. 全面掌握包装函写作的要领。
2. 学习包装函写作的常用词组、典型句式。
3. 学习包装函写作的专业术语。
4. 学习包装函写作的商务背景知识。

能力目标: 1. 能够熟练运用本环节所学习的专业术语、常用词组、典型句式正确撰写包装函。
2. 掌握包装函写作所需要的相关商务背景知识。

任务: Zukov公司发现合同中关于包装的条款不是非常明确清晰,因此致信鲁农公司,再次明确包装相关的条款和包装要求,强调务必按照要求对产品进行认真的包装。

请就此撰写一封包装指示函。

要求如下:
1. 强调包装必须符合长途海运的要求。
2. 强调包装要防潮。

你可以借助资料库中的相关资料来撰写包装指示函。

范例:

案例4 向俄罗斯Zukov公司出口苹果

Jun. 20, 2015

Dear Mr. Liu,

After going through the contract, we find that the packing clause is not clear enough and we have to reiterate that the relative clause should read as follows.

Packing should be seaworthy packing suitable for long distance marine transportation.

The goods must be well protected against moisture.

We look forward to hearing from you.

Yours sincerely

Yuri Barsherv

学习情境8：保险函（Correspondence for Insurance）

知识目标： 1. 全面掌握保险函写作的要领。
2. 学习保险函写作的常用词组、典型句式。
3. 学习保险函写作的专业术语。
4. 学习保险函写作的商务背景知识。

能力目标： 1. 能够熟练运用本环节所学习的专业术语、常用词组、典型句式正确撰写保险函。
2. 掌握保险函写作所需要的相关商务背景知识。

任务： 经过多方努力后，鲁农公司终于完成了商品的生产任务，致信Zukov，要求其为相关商品购买保险。但是Zukov希望鲁农公司能够代为投保。

请就此撰写一封要求卖方代为购买保险的请求函。

要求如下：

1. 请求鲁农公司按发票金额的110%代为购买一切险。
2. 承诺收到账单后会立即付还鲁农公司所垫付的保费。

你可以借助资料库中的相关资料来撰写保险函。

范例:

July. 10, 2015

Dear Mr. Liu,

We are so glad that the production has been successfully completed and do appreciate your efforts. As we desire to have the goods insured at your end, would you please insure the consignment on our behalf against All Risks for 110% of the invoice value. We shall refund the premium immediately upon receipt of your debit note.

Your approval would be highly appreciated and if you have any further instructions, please do not hesitate to contact us.

Yours sincerely

Barsherv

学习情境9:运输函(Correspondence for Shipment)

知识目标:1. 全面掌握运输函写作的要领。
    2. 学习运输函写作的常用词组、典型句式。
    3. 学习运输函写作的专业术语。
    4. 学习运输函写作的商务背景知识。

能力目标:1. 能够熟练运用本环节所学习的专业术语、常用词组、典型句式正确撰写运输函。
    2. 掌握运输函写作所需要的相关商务背景知识。

任务:Zukov按照合同规定,在货轮Greatania上预定了仓位。近期收到了轮船公司通知,Greatania将在9月10日左右从青岛港起航。ThoMron公司给鲁农公司发出了通知。请就此撰写一封告知对方起运时间的通知函。

案例4 向俄罗斯Zukov公司出口苹果

要求如下：
1. 告知对方起运时间。
2. 要求对方尽快完成装运工作。

你可以借助资料库中的相关资料来撰写通知函。

范例：

July 20, 2015

Dear Mr. Liu Qiang,

We have been informed by the shipping company that S/S Greatania is due to sail from Qingdao Port on or about September 10, on which we have booked room for the smartphones.

We would like you to arrange shipment of the goods with least possible delay.

Your close cooperation in this respect will be highly appreciated.

Sincerely yours

Yuri Barsherv

学习情境10：索赔和纠纷解决
(Correspondence for Claim and Settlement)

知识目标：1. 全面掌握索赔函写作的要领。
　　　　　2. 学习索赔函写作的常用词组、典型句式。
　　　　　3. 学习索赔函写作的专业术语。
　　　　　4. 学习索赔函写作的商务背景知识。
能力目标：1. 能够熟练运用本环节所学习的专业术语、常用词组、典型句式正确撰写索赔函。
　　　　　2. 掌握索赔函写作所需要的相关商务背景知识。

任务：经过两个多月的长途海运后，鲁农公司的货物终于顺利抵达圣彼得堡港。但是 Zukov 公司验收货物时，发现有一个货盘内的苹果干包装出现破损，因此提出索赔。

请就此撰写一封索赔函。

要求如下：
1. 告知鲁农公司货物已收到。
2. 告知对方有一个货盘的苹果干包装破损，因此要求赔偿 1 万美元。

你可以借助资料库中的相关资料来撰写索赔函。

范例：

Oct. 10, 2015

Dear Mr. Liu Qiang,

We have received the ordered goods, but we were surprised and disappointed to find after careful examination that the package in one ballet is broken which surely has contaminated the apple chips in it.

You can see that this accident no doubt will affect our sales seriously and we have to ask you US $ 10000 for compensation.

We are looking forward to a satisfactory conclusion of this problem.

Yours respectfully

Yuri Barsherv

任务：经过公司紧急调查，鲁农公司发现的确是由于自己的失误，造成包装受损，因此致函 Zukov，告知其调查结果和公司的解决方案。

请就此撰写一封索赔回复函。

要求如下：
1. 告知 Zukov，经过公司调查，的确有一货盘的包装受损。
2. 公司对此提出两个解决方案：立刻将 1 货盘通过空运直接送往圣彼得堡，或者提供

7000 美元的特别折扣。

你可以借助资料库中的相关资料来撰写索赔回复函。

范例：

Oct. 25, 2015

Dear Mr. Barsherv,

Our investigation sadly confirms your complaints. We are very sorry for this accident and sincerely apologize for it.

To solve the problem, we suggest that we either send another ballet by air freight directly to St. Petersburg on our expense or pay you 7000 as special allowance.

Please accept our sincere apology and we look forward to your decision as to which is preferable to you.

Sincerely yours

Liu Qiang

商业背景知识拓展

1. Introduction of Russian Economy

In 2015, the Russian economy was the sixth largest in the world and twelfth largest at market exchange rates. In January 2016, Russia's economy was rated by Bloomberg as the 12th most innovative in the world. Russia has the world's 15th highest patent application rate, the 8th highest concentration of high-tech public companies, such as internet and aerospace and the third highest graduation rate of scientists and engineers.

Russia has a mixed economy with state ownership in strategic areas of the economy. Although market reforms in the 1990s privatized much of Russian industry and agriculture, energy and defense-related sectors are mostly still owned by the state.

It is estimated that Russia contains over 30 percent of the world's natural resources, whose total value is around $75 trillion US dollars. The country relies on energy revenues to drive most of its growth. Russia has an abundance of oil, natural gas and precious metals, which make up a major share of Russia's exports.

Between 2000 and 2012 Russia's energy exports fueled a rapid growth in living standards. In the same period, unemployment and poverty more than halved and Russians' self-assessed life satisfaction also rose significantly. This growth was a combined result of the 2000s commodities boom, high oil prices, as well as prudent economic and fiscal policies. These gains, however, have been distributed unevenly, as the 110 wealthiest individuals own 35% of all financial assets held by Russian households. Russia also has the second-largest volume of illicit money outflows, having lost over $880 billion between 2002 and 2011 in this way.

2. E-commerce Boosting Russia-China Trade

China's cross-border e-commerce trade has been developing rapidly, which will help create jobs and inject new energy into the economy. More than 80 percent of Chinese foreign trade firms have an online-business arm. E-commerce between Russia and China has grown rapidly and Russia is one of the most attractive markets for China's foreign trade firms which have committed to advancing bilateral e-commerce cooperation.

According to China Internet Network Information Center, the country had 649 million Internet users by the end of 2014, and some 557 million used mobile phones to get online. The digital era has helped bring cheaper Russian goods, especially organic food, such as flour, honey, beer, vegetable oil and fruit juice featured prominently. On

Singles' Day of 2013, the global shopping festival launched by e-commerce giant Alibaba Group Holding Ltd on Nov. 11, Russian customers purchased the largest amount of goods among overseas buyers. Around 300 million packages containing items bought on the Internet were transported from China to Russia. That increased to more than 700 million in 2014, and hit more than 1 billion by the end of 2015. The economists have forecasted that if the two countries continue to nurture the right conditions for trade investment growth, it is likely to reach ＄200 billion by 2020.

"E-commerce is significant in integrating traditional and emerging industries, reducing logistics costs, encouraging entrepreneurship, creating jobs and boosting consumption," a government statement said.

案例 5　向印度尼西亚 Maluka 公司出口计算机

商业背景设定：

出口商：北京华威计算机有限公司（Beijing Huawei Computer Company），中国最大的计算机制造企业之一，公司生产和销售多种型号的台式和笔记本计算机。公司技术力量雄厚，在计算机研发、外观设计、售后服务等方面均有良好的口碑。

公司地址：中国北京市朝阳区西大望路 1366 号

总经理：朱威

主要产品：台式计算机、笔记本计算机

进口商：Maluka 公司系印度尼西亚知名的计算机进口和销售商，其营销网络覆盖了印度尼西亚、泰国、马来西亚、越南等东南亚国家，年营业额超过 20 亿美元。

公司地址：539 M. H. Thamrin Street. , Jakarta

总经理：罗斯·木雅缇（Ros Mulyati）

华威公司的产品长期以内销为主，在国内市场具有较高的知名度和份额。但是随着中国计算机制造厂商的增多，国内市场竞争日趋激烈，华威公司的市场份额逐年下降。为了应对这一严峻的局面，华威公司积极响应国家"走出去"的战略，决定大力开发国际市场。公司认为东南亚国家人口众多，与中国贸易联系紧密，潜力巨大，因此决定将公司产品推向印度尼西亚市场，力争能够以此为着力点，逐步占领东南亚市场。

华威公司通过中国驻印度尼西亚商务参赞处获得了 Maluka 公司希望与中国企业合作进行计算机进口业务的信息。华威公司还从参赞处得知该公司实力雄厚，营销网络发达，诚实守信，因此在东南亚地区有较高的知名度。华威公司据此判断，Maluka 是符合其战略转型的理想合作伙伴。

学习情境 1：建交函
（Correspondence for Establishing Business Relations）

知识目标：1. 全面掌握建交函写作的要领。

2. 学习建交函写作的常用词组、典型句式。

3. 学习建交函写作的专业术语。

4. 学习建交函写作的商务背景知识。

能力目标： 1. 能够熟练运用本环节所学习的专业术语、常用词组、典型句式正确撰写建交函。
2. 掌握建交函写作所需要的相关商务背景知识。

任务： 华威公司总经理朱威给 Maluka 公司总经理 Mulyati 先生发出一封建交函，表达与对方合作的意愿，并且希望早日得到回复。

请就此撰写一封建交函。

要求如下：
1. 介绍本公司基本情况。
2. 表达合作意愿。

你可以借助资料库中的相关资料来撰写建交函。

范例：

Huawei Computer Company
No. 1366 Xidawang Road,
Chaoyang District, Beijing
P. R. China
Jan. 20, 2015

Maluka
539 M. H. Thamrin Street,
Jakarta, Indonesia

Dear Mr. Mulyati,

We learn from the Commercial Counsellor's Office of our Embassy in your country that you are one of the biggest importer of computer in Indonesia.

As one of the key computer producers in China, we produce high quality desktop computer and notebook computer that enjoy great popularity in the Chinese market. We believe our products can meet perfectly the demands of your clients and have the pleasure of addressing this letter to you in the hope of establishing business relations with you.

Enclosed you will find a copy of our catalogue for your reference and hope that you would contact us if you are interested in any item.

We are looking forward to hearing from you soon.

Sincerely yours

Zhu Wei

General Manager

学习情境2：询盘函（Correspondence for Enquiry）

知识目标： 1. 全面掌握询盘函写作的要领。
2. 学习询盘函的常用词组、典型句式。
3. 学习询盘函写作的专业术语。
4. 学习询盘函写作的商务背景知识。

能力目标： 1. 能够熟练运用本环节所学习的专业术语、常用词组、典型句式正确撰写询盘函。
2. 掌握询盘函写作所需要的相关商务背景知识。

任务： Maluka 公司正在积极拓宽供货渠道从而降低成本，因此非常重视华威公司建立贸易关系的来函。Maluka 公司通过调查，确认华威公司是一家实力雄厚的中国企业，其产品质量较为可靠，有较高的信用度。华威公司寄来的产品目录中有一款最新推出的笔记本计算机 TXE – 966，它引起了 Maluka 公司的高度关注，认为这个产品设计新颖，功能强大，非常适合印度尼西亚消费者的需求，因此决定和华威公司进行贸易联系。Mulyati 先生回函朱威总经理，感谢华威公司的来信，表达合作意愿并请华威公司寄送样品。

请就此撰写一封要求寄送样品的询盘函。

要求如下：
1. 感谢对方来电，表明公司希望双方能够紧密合作。
2. 要求寄送 5 台型号为 TXE – 966 的笔记本计算机。

你可以借助资料库中的相关资料来撰写询盘函。

范例：

Jan. 30, 2015

Dear Mr. Zhu,

Thank you for your letter of Jan. 20 and we note with pleasure that you intend to develop business with us.

We have gone through your catalogue and are interested in notebook TXE-966. Please send us 5 notebooks for further inspection and if the quality is satisfactory, we shall consider placing an order.

We await your prompt reply.

Sincerely yours

Mulyati

President

　　任务： 华威公司收到要求寄送样品的回复函后，在最短的时间内将客户所要求的5台TXE-966笔记本计算机发送到Maluka公司。Maluka公司对这些样品进行了检测和研究，认为其质量完全符合公司的标准，且外观设计非常新颖，可以满足印度尼西亚消费者的需求，因此决定与华威公司开展进口业务。Mulyati先生致函朱威总经理，告知对方计划订购TXE-966笔记本计算机1000台，要求华威公司对该批货物报价。

　　请就此撰写一封要求报价的询盘函。
　　要求如下：
　　1. 对寄送样品表示满意，要订购1000台TXE-966笔记本计算机。
　　2. 请求华威公司报FOB天津价。

你可以借助资料库中的相关资料来撰写询盘函。

范例：

Feb. 20, 2015

Dear Mr. Zhu,

Thank you for your samples which have been passed our quality test and we believe your computer will be popular in our market.

Please quote us your lowest possible FOB Tianjing price for 1000 computers. The order will be placed if your price is reasonable.

Your early reply is highly appreciated.

Sincerely yours

Ros Mulyati

学习情境3：发盘函（Correspondence for Offers）

知识目标：1. 全面掌握发盘函写作的要领。
　　　　　2. 学习发盘函写作的常用词组、典型句式。
　　　　　3. 学习发盘函写作的专业术语。
　　　　　4. 学习发盘函写作的商务背景知识。

能力目标：1. 能够熟练运用本环节所学习的专业术语、常用词组、典型句式正确撰写发盘函。
　　　　　2. 掌握发盘函写作所需要的相关商务背景知识。

　　任务：华威公司收到Maluka公司的询盘函后，经过认真的研究，认为应该先向Maluka公司发出一个虚盘，这样可以在今后的谈判过程中争取主动。
　　请就此撰写一封发盘函。

案例5　向印度尼西亚Maluka公司出口计算机

要求如下：

品名：TXE-966 笔记本计算机

价格：FOB 天津价，每台 800 美元

数量：1000 台

包装：10 台装 1 木箱

交货期：2015 年 6 月

支付方式：不可撤销即期汇票信用证

你可以借助资料库中的相关资料来撰写发盘函。

范例：

Mar. 10, 2015

Dear Mr. Mulyati,

In reply to your letter of Feb 20, we have pleasure in offering, subject to our final confirmation. We are pleased to quote as follows.

  Commodity：TXE-966 Notebook
  Price：US $ 800 per set, FOB Tianjin
  Quantity：1000 sets
  Packing：10 sets in a wooden case
  Shipment：in June, 2015
  Payment：by irrevocable L/C, payable by draft at sight

We hope this offer will be of interest to you and are looking forward to your favorable reply.

Yours faithfully

zhu wei

学习情境 4：还盘函（Correspondence for Counter-offers）

知识目标： 1. 全面掌握还盘函写作的要领。
2. 学习还盘函写作的常用词组、典型句式。
3. 学习还盘函写作的专业术语。
4. 学习还盘函写作的商务背景知识。

能力目标： 1. 能够熟练运用本环节所学习的专业术语、常用词组、典型句式正确撰写还盘函。
2. 掌握还盘函写作所需要的相关商务背景知识。

任务： Maluka 收到华威公司的报价后，认为华威公司的计算机产品从未在印度尼西亚尼市场上销售过，还没有建立起顾客口碑，如果按当前的报价，可能会影响消费者的购买意愿，因此致函朱威总经理，希望华威公司降低价格。

请就此撰写一封还盘函。

要求如下：

1. 告知华威公司报价偏高。
2. 希望计算机的价格能降到 700 美元/台。

你可以借助资料库中的相关资料来撰写还盘函。

范例：

Mar. 21, 2015

Dear Mr. Zhu,

We have received your offer of Feb. 20 for TXE – 966 Notebook with many thanks.

All the terms in this offer are acceptable except the price. Although the quality and design of your product are impressive, but since you are new in the Indonesian market, our customers might consider this price too high. A lower price will be more competitive and attract more customers, which is helpful to win the share of market for your product in the long run. Therefore, we would like to place an order with you if you could reduce your price to US $ 700 per set. Should this deal prove successful, you can expect more substantial orders.

Your consideration of our suggestion will be appreciated.

Yours faithfully

Ros Mulyati

Maluka

任务：华威公司认真研究并测算了 Maluka 的还价，认为 700 美元/台的价格是可以接受的，因此决定接受 Maluka 公司对于计算机的还价。
请就此撰写一封还盘函。
要求如下：
1. 对 Maluka 公司给出的不能接受的报价的解释表示理解。
2. 说明为了今后的合作，同意将计算机的价格降至 700 美元/台。
3. 告知对方此价格为最终报价。

你可以借助资料库中的相关资料来撰写还盘函。

范例：

Mar. 30, 2015

Dear Mr. Mulyati,

Your kind explanation of rejecting our offer is received with understanding although we are disappointed and still believe our price is reasonable. However, bearing in mind of the special demand of a new market, we agree to your suggestion to our price of notebook to 700 dollars/set.

We must stress that this offer is the lowest possible one and your prompt reply would be highly appreciated.

Yours faithfully

Zhu Wei

付款方式诈骗案例

Y公司向美国Z公司出口工艺品。第一笔交易中Z公司坚持要求以T/T方式付款,称这样节约费用对双方有利。考虑双方长时间交往,Y公司答应了客户的要求。Y公司收到B/L后即发传真给Z公司。对方很快将货款汇给Y公司。不久后Z公司再次向Y公司购买工艺品,并要求T/T付款,由于第一单非常顺利,Y公司同意其要求。随后三个月内连续4次返单,由于Y公司放松警惕,既没有及时追要货款,更没有采取任何措施,使Z公司在没有正本B/L的情况下从运输公司轻松提货。当Y公司在四批货物全部出运后再向Z公司索款时,对方以各种理由拖延,不久后Z公司人去楼空,传真、E-MAIL不通,造成Y公司损失高达数十万美元。

学习情境5:订单函(Correspondence for Orders)

知识目标: 1. 全面掌握订单函写作的要领。
2. 学习订单函写作的常用词组、典型句式。
3. 学习订单函写作的专业术语。
4. 学习订单函写作的商务背景知识。

能力目标: 1. 能够熟练运用本环节所学习的专业术语、常用词组、典型句式正确撰写订单函。
2. 掌握订单函写作所需要的相关商务背景知识。

任务: Maluka公司对于华威公司的积极合作态度非常欣赏,因此决定下订单,并且主动提出将订单从1000台增加到1500台,以此来表示自己对于今后进一步开展贸易往来的热切期望和真诚合作的态度。

请就此撰写一封订单函。
要求如下:
品名:TXE-966笔记本计算机
价格:FOB天津价,每台700美元
数量:1500台
包装:10台装1木箱
交货期:2015年6月
支付方式:不可撤销即期汇票信用证

案例5 向印度尼西亚Maluka公司出口计算机

你可以借助资料库中的相关资料来撰写订单函。

范例：

April 10, 2015

Dear Mr. Zhu,

We are pleased in sending you the order confirmation covering our purchase from you of TXE-966 Notebook. We increase the quantity from 1000 to 1500 sets to demonstrate our sincerity for cooperation. Our order is as follows.

    Commodity: TXE-966 Notebook
    Price: US $800 per set,
          FOB Tianjin
    Quantity: 1500 sets
    Packing: 10 sets in a wooden case
    Shipment: in June, 2015
    Payment: by irrevocable L/C, payable by draft at sight

If the execution of the first order turns out to our satisfaction, we will place repeat order in the near future.

Sincerely yours

Ros Mulyati

学习情境6：支付方式函（Correspondence for Term of Payment）

知识目标：1. 全面掌握支付方式函写作的要领。
          2. 学习支付方式函写作的常用词组、典型句式。
          3. 学习支付方式函写作的专业术语。
          4. 学习支付方式函写作的商务背景知识。

能力目标： 1. 能够熟练运用本环节所学习的专业术语、常用词组、典型句式正确撰写支付方式函。
2. 掌握支付方式函写作所需要的相关商务背景知识。

任务： 按照双方签署的销售合同，Maluka 公司应该在 4 月 10 日之前将其在银行开立信用证寄送至华威公司，但是直到 4 月 25 日，华威公司仍然没有收到 Maluka 公司的信用证。
请就此撰写一封催促开立信用证通知函。
要求如下：
1. 告知 Maluka 本公司尚未收到应该在 4 月 10 日前寄送到达的信用证。
2. 提请 Maluka 尽快开立信用证，否则会影响装运时间。

你可以借助资料库中的相关资料来撰写开立信用证通知函。

范例：

April 25, 2015

Dear Mr. Mulgati,

Subject: Establishment of L/C for TXE – 966 Notebook

Much to our regret, we have not receive your L/C against our order of TXE – 966 notebook computers. This letter, as we understand according to our agreement should have reached us by April 10.

We will have to delay the time of shipment if you do not expedite the establishment of the L/C concerned and send it to us before the end of this month.

Yours faithfully

Zhu Wei

任务： 华威公司终于在 5 月 3 日收到了 Maluka 公司开立的信用证，但是审证后发现信用证与销售合同的条款有不符之处，因此致函 Maluka 公司要求其进行修改。

请就此撰写一封信用证修改的通知函。
要求如下：
1. 说明信用证与合同有不符之处。
2. 指出信用证中订购量为 1000 台而非合同中约定的 1500 台。
3. 指出包装应为"10 台计算机装一箱"，而非信用证中的"20 台计算机装一箱"。

你可以借助资料库中的相关资料来撰写更改支付方式请求函。

范例：

May 5, 2015

Dear Mr. Mulyati,

Thank you for your L/C No. 21489 which reached us yesterday. However, when we checked it with the sales contract, we were very sorry to tell you that two amendments should be made in the following points:
    1. The quantity of the commodity should be "1500 sets" as stipulated in the sales contract.
    2. The packing clause in your L/C should read "10 sets in a wooden case" instead of "20 sets in a wooden case".

Please amend your credit as soon as possible since the shipment has been delayed due to its late arrival.

Sincerely yours

Zhu Wei

常用付款方式的风险分析

O/A（Open Account）：赊销。该种方式通常是交易双方达成协议，由卖方先行向买方发运货物，货款一季、半年或一年结算。此支付方式属于商业信用，出口方是否能够安全收到款项，完全基于进口方的信用。

学习情境7：包装函（Correspondence for Packing）

知识目标：1. 全面掌握包装函写作的要领。
2. 学习包装函写作的常用词组、典型句式。
3. 学习包装函写作的专业术语。
4. 学习包装函写作的商务背景知识。

能力目标：1. 能够熟练运用本环节所学习的专业术语、常用词组、典型句式正确撰写包装函。
2. 掌握包装函写作所需要的相关商务背景知识。

任务：Maluka公司按照合同要求在"龙运号"货轮上为进口的计算机预订好了舱位，同时致信华威公司，再次明确包装相关的条款和包装要求，强调务必按照要求对产品进行认真的包装。

请就此撰写一封包装指示函。
要求如下：
1. 要求用防水纸包裹计算机。
2. 强调包装箱上开通风孔。
3. 要求箱子的主标志需注明毛重、净重、目的港、原产国。

你可以借助资料库中的相关资料来撰写包装指示函。

范例：

Jun. 20, 2015

Dear Mr. Zhu,

Subject: Seaworthy Packing Suitable For Long Distance Marine Transportation.

We have booked space on S/S Longyun for the goods and we consider it important and necessary to reiterate some of the packing requirements to eliminate any future trouble since this is the first time we import computers from China.
1. The computers should be wrapped closely before being placed into the wooden case, and vent holes should be cut to minimize condensation.

2. The main shipping mark should demonstrate the gross and net weight, port of destination and country of origin.

We look forward to hearing from you.

Yours sincerely

Ros Mulyati

学习情境8：保险函（Correspondence for Insurance）

知识目标： 1. 全面掌握保险函写作的要领。
2. 学习保险函写作的常用词组、典型句式。
3. 学习保险函写作的专业术语。
4. 学习保险函写作的商务背景知识。

能力目标： 1. 能够熟练运用本环节所学习的专业术语、常用词组、典型句式正确撰写保险函。
2. 掌握保险函写作所需要的相关商务背景知识。

任务： 按照合同要求，Maluka公司应该为此批进口计算机购买保险，公司为此致电中国华商保险公司，询问从天津港到雅加达港的保险费率。

请就此撰写一封保险费率征询函。

要求如下：

1. 说明保险货物、货物价值、装运货轮、起止区间。
2. 说明保险品种。

你可以借助资料库中的相关资料来撰写保险函。

范例：

July 10, 2015

Sino-merchants Insurance Company
No. 22 Jianguo Road

Beijing, China

Dear Sirs,

We are writing to inquire about your insurance rate as we are going to transport 1500 notebook computers from Tianjin Port to Port of Jakarta. The goods is valued at US＄1050000 and will be on S/S Longyun before the end of July.

We should be pleased if you would quote us for All Risks as soon as possible.

Yours sincerely

Ros Mulyati

学习情境9：运输函（Correspondence for Shipment）

知识目标：1. 全面掌握运输函写作的要领。
2. 学习运输函写作的常用词组、典型句式。
3. 学习运输函写作的专业术语。
4. 学习运输函写作的商务背景知识。

能力目标：1. 能够熟练运用本环节所学习的专业术语、常用词组、典型句式正确撰写运输函。
2. 掌握运输函写作所需要的相关商务背景知识。

任务：华威公司按照合同规定，准时将出口货物运送至天津码头。在所有货物顺利装运上Maluka公司指定的货轮"龙运号"后，华威公司致信Maluka，告知其装运完毕，并且附上装运单据。

请就此撰写一封告知对方装运完成的通知函。

要求如下：

1. 告知对方装运完成时间。
2. 告知对方轮船起航时间。
3. 告知对方随函附上装运单据，其中包括不可转让提单、签署好的发票、装箱单、原产地证明、保险单等。

你可以借助资料库中的相关资料来撰写通知函。

范例:

July 20, 2015

Dear Mr. RosMulyati,

We are pleased to inform you that the shipment has been made on July 19 on S/S Longyun at Tianjin Port. We were told by the transporter that the ship is due to leave Tianjin on or about July 25.

Enclosed kindly find the duplicate shipping documents which include:
    a. A non-negotiable copy of bill of lading
    b. A signed invoice
    c. Packing list
    d. Certificate of Origin
    e. Insurance policy

We are happy to have filled your order on time and sure the goods will you're your demands.

Sincerely yours

Zhu Wei

学习情境10:索赔和纠纷解决
(Correspondence for Claim and Settlement)

知识目标:1. 全面掌握索赔函写作的要领。
    2. 学习索赔函写作的常用词组、典型句式。
    3. 学习索赔函写作的专业术语。
    4. 学习索赔函写作的商务背景知识。

能力目标：1. 能够熟练运用本环节所学习的专业术语、常用词组、典型句式正确撰写索赔函。
2. 掌握索赔函写作所需要的相关商务背景知识。

任务：一个月后，Maluka 公司收到了订购的笔记本计算机。但是在验收货物时，发现计算机少运来 50 台，因此向华威公司提出索赔。

请就此撰写一封索赔函。

要求如下：
1. 告知计算机少了 50 台。
2. 要求赔偿 3.5 万美元。

你可以借助资料库中的相关资料来撰写索赔函。

范例：

August 10, 2015

Dear Mr. Zhu Wei,

The computers have arrived at the Port of Jakarta. While appreciating your prompt shipment, we found with regrets that the number of the notebook computers is 1450 instead of 1500 as we ordered.

We reserve the right to lodge a claim of US $35000 on you for the shortage and your serious and prompt consideration to this matter are expected.

We are looking forward to a satisfactory conclusion of this problem.

Yours respectfully

Ros Mulyati

　　任务：经过调查，华威公司发现自己完全按照合同要求将 1500 台计算机装箱并装运上货轮，因此对于货物的缺失不应承担任何责任。

案例5　向印度尼西亚 Maluka 公司出口计算机

请就此撰写一封索赔回复函。
要求如下：
1. 告知 Maluka，经过公司调查，装运的计算机数量与合同完全相符。
2. 建议对方向轮船公司或者保险公司联系赔偿事宜。

你可以借助资料库中的相关资料来撰写索赔回复函。

范例：

August 25, 2015

Dear Mr. Mulyati,

We are sorry for the shortage of goods, but after serious investigation, we found that the number of computers we sent to the ship was in accordance with the number in the contract. Therefore, we can only conclude that the shortage happened during the transit, for which we should not be held responsible.

We advise you to contact the forwarding agent or insurance company for compensation.

Sincerely yours

Zhu Wei

商业背景知识拓展

1. Introduction of Indonesian Economy

Indonesia is the sixteenth largest economy in the world and has the largest economy in Southeast Asia. As one of the emerging market economies of the world, the country is also a member of G – 20 major economies and classified as a newly industrialised country. Indonesian economy depends heavily on domestic market, and government budget spending and its ownership of state-owned enterprises and the administration of prices of a range of basic goods including fuel, rice, and electricity plays a significant role in Indonesia market economy.

Since the late 1980s, Indonesia has made significant changes to its regulatory framework to encourage economic growth. This growth was financed largely from private investment, both foreign and domestic. US investors dominated the oil and gas sector and undertook some of Indonesia's largest mining projects. In addition, the presence of US banks, manufacturers, and service providers expanded, especially after the industrial and financial sector reforms of the 1980s. Other major foreign investors included India, Japan, the United Kingdom, Singapore, the Netherlands, Qatar and South Korea.

The economic crisis that began in mid - 1997 made continued private financing imperative but problematic. New foreign investment approvals fell by almost two-thirds between 1997 and 1999. The crisis further highlighted areas where additional reform was needed. Frequently-cited areas for improving the investment climate were establishment of a functioning legal and judicial system, adherence to competitive processes, and adoption of internationally acceptable accounting and disclosure standards. Despite improvements in the laws in recent years, Indonesia's intellectual property rights regime remains weak; lack of effective enforcement is a major concern.

2. Closer Economic Relationship between China and Indonesia

In 2003 trade between Indonesia and China reached only US＄3.8 billion, in 2010 it multiplied almost 10 times. China's transformation into a major economic power in the 21st century has led to an increase of foreign investments in the bamboo network, a network of overseas Chinese businesses operating in the markets of Southeast Asia that share common family and cultural ties.

China has been one of Indonesia's key major trading partners in recent years, serving as the country's largest export and import market. By 2010, China had managed to overtake the United States as Indonesia's second-largest export destination after Japan.

China is also becoming Indonesia's most important source of imports, reaching US $19.6 billion in 2010. The balance however was in favor of China as Indonesia booked trade deficit US $ -4.7 billion in 2010. Some Indonesian economists doubt the trade with China, believing that the inflows of cheap products from China could harm Indonesian industry. Indonesian private sector and civil society organizations vigorously lobbied the Indonesian government and members of parliament, insisting that Indonesia should either pull out of the agreement or renegotiate its terms with Beijing.

From China's perspective, since 2010 ASEAN as a whole has become its fourth-largest trading partner after the European Union, Japan and the United States. Among ASEAN member countries, Indonesia was China's fourth-largest trading partner after Malaysia, Singapore and Thailand.

On late September 2015, Indonesia awards multibillion-dollar Jakarta-Bandung high-speed railway project to China. It was said that China's offer to build the Jakarta-Bandung line without requiring loan guarantee nor funding from Indonesia was the tipping point of Jakarta's decision. The Jakarta-Bandung high-speed rail is planned to begin its operations to public in 2019.

第二部分 进口业务

案例 1 从法国 Lancelot 公司进口化妆品

商业背景设定：

进口商：风华公司（Fenghua Beauty Maker），中国知名美容院连锁集团。
公司地址：中国上海市霞飞路 125 号
总经理：刘珊
主要产品：高档美容服务

出口商：Lancelot，法国最大的化妆品生产销售公司之一，产品系列丰富，质量上乘，在国际市场享有盛誉。
公司地址：221 Ponpiduelei Boulevard, Paris
董事长：Antony Genei

美容、化妆行业，尤其是其高端业态在中国发展势头强劲，市场竞争日趋激烈。高质量的产品和高质量的服务是商家立于不败之地的法宝，风华公司为了能在高端美容市场占得先机，决定从国外寻找合适的生意伙伴，引进高级化妆品。通过认真深入的市场调研，风华公司认为法国的高端化妆品在全世界都有着非常高的知名度，因此决定将合作伙伴设定法国公司。与此同时，作为化妆品的重要生产国和出口国，很多法国化妆品公司也将中国视为最有潜力的巨大市场，希望拓展中国业务。著名的化妆品生产商 Lancelot 就向风华公司发来了建交函。

复习情境 1：建交函
(Correspondence for Establishing Business Relations)

知识目标：1. 巩固与操练建交函写作的要领。
　　　　　2. 复习建交函写作的常用词组、典型句式。

3. 复习建交函写作的专业术语。
4. 复习建交函写作的商务背景知识。

能力目标： 1. 能够熟练运用本环节所复习的专业术语、常用词组、典型句式正确撰写建交函。
2. 巩固与操练建交函写作所需要的相关商务背景知识。

任务： Lancelot 公司向风华公司发出一封建交函，表达与其合作的意愿，希望早日得到回复。

请就此撰写一封建交函。

要求如下：
1. 介绍 Lancelot 公司的基本情况。
2. 表达合作意愿。

你可以借助资料库中的相关资料来撰写建交函。

范例：

Fenghua Beauty Maker
No. 125 Xiafei Street,
Shanghai, P. R. China
Jan. 20, 2015

Lancelot
221 Ponpiduelei Boulevard
Paris, France

Dear Sirs,

We have got your name and address from your advertisement and have the pleasure to introduce ourselves to you with a view to establish business relations with your company.

We are a famous French cosmetic producer and our products are popular with the high end customers in America, Europe and Asia for their great quality. Presently we are keen to expand our business in China.

Enclosed please find our latest illustrated catalogue and price list. Should you require any further details about our company, please do not hesitate to contact us.

We look forward to your early reply.

Sincerely yours

Antony Genei

General Manager

复习情境2：询盘函（Correspondence for Enquiry）

知识目标：1. 巩固与操练询盘函写作的要领。
2. 复习询盘函的常用词组、典型句式。
3. 复习询盘函写作的专业术语。
4. 复习询盘函写作的商务背景知识。

能力目标：1. 能够熟练运用本环节所复习的专业术语、常用词组、典型句式正确撰写询盘函。
2. 巩固与操练询盘函写作所需要的相关商务背景知识。

任务：风华公司认为Lancelot作为法国最大的化妆品生产销售公司之一，其产品在国际市场享有盛誉，非常受中国高端用户的欢迎，因此与Lancelot公司建立合作关系。刘珊总经理回函Lancelot公司总经理，对其来信表示感谢，同时希望能给风华公司寄送样品。

请就此撰写一封要求寄送样品的询盘函。
要求如下：
1. 感谢对方来电。
2. 要求寄送样品，包括Voloet眼霜、Frangrant日霜和晚霜、Votrovlet香水各五瓶。

你可以借助资料库中的相关资料来撰写询盘函。

范例：

案例1 从法国Lancelot公司进口化妆品

Jan. 30, 2015

Dear Mr. Genei,

We are very pleased to have received your letter of Jan. 20.

As you may know, the market for luxurious cosmetics is growing swiftly in China and as one of the biggest providers of plastic surgery service, we are very interested in building close relationship with a prestigious company from France like you. To get the first-hand feedback from our customers about your products, we would like you to send us some samples and our requests are as follows: Voloet eye cream, Frangrant day cream and night cream, Votrovlet perfume, five bottles for each item. We are more than happy to place an order with you if your products prove satisfactory.

Your prompt and favorable reply is highly expected.

Sincerely yours

Liu Shan

任务：Lancelot 公司很快就按风华公司的要求寄来了样品。通过客户试用和反馈，风华公司对于寄来的样品非常满意，刘珊总经理致信 Genei 先生，告知对方计划首批购买 Voloet 眼霜 200 瓶、Frangrant 日霜和晚霜各 200 瓶、Votrovlet 香水 200 瓶，要求 Lancelot 公司进行报价。

请就此撰写一封要求报价的询盘函。

要求如下：

1. 对寄送样品表示满意。
2. 告知对方计划订购 Voloet 眼霜 200 瓶、Frangrant 日霜和晚霜各 200 瓶、Votrovlet 香水 200 瓶。
3. 请求 Lancelot 公司对此进行报价。

你可以借助资料库中的相关资料来撰写询盘函。

范例：

Feb. 20, 2015

Dear Mr. Genei,

Thank you for your prompt delivery of the samples. We are glad to inform you that the customers' comments on your products are very positive and we are very satisfied with your products. For the first order, we would like to place an order of Voloet eye cream, Frangrant day cream and night cream, Votrovlet perfume, 200 bottles for each item. Please quote us the details of your price and terms of payment. Should your price and quality be found reasonable, we will soon place more orders.

Your early offer will be highly appreciated.

Sincerely yours

Liu Shan

复习情境3：发盘函（Correspondence for Offers）

知识目标： 1. 巩固与操练发盘函写作的要领。
2. 复习发盘函写作的常用词组、典型句式。
3. 复习发盘函写作的专业术语。
4. 复习发盘函写作的商务背景知识。

能力目标： 1. 能够熟练运用本环节所复习的专业术语、常用词组、典型句式正确撰写发盘函。
2. 巩固与操练发盘函写作所需要的相关商务背景知识。

任务： 收到风华公司的询价信后，Lancelot公司为能够找到这样理想的合作伙伴感到非常高兴，因此迅速向其发盘。

请就此撰写一封发盘函。

要求如下：

品名：Voloet eye cream

单价：每瓶100欧元，FOB马赛

数量：200瓶

案例1 从法国Lancelot公司进口化妆品

品名：Frangrant day cream
单价：每瓶 150 欧元，FOB 马赛
数量：200 瓶

品名：Frangrant night cream
单价：每瓶 150 欧元，FOB 马赛
数量：200 瓶

品名：Votrovlet perfume
单价：每瓶 150 欧元，FOB 马赛
数量：200 瓶

包装：泡沫塑料包裹，50 瓶装入一木箱
交货期：收到信用证后 4 周内发货
保险：由买方投保
支付方式：不可撤销的见票即付信用证

你可以借助资料库中的相关资料来撰写发盘函。

范例：

Mar. 10, 2015

Dear Ms. Liu,

Your letter has been received with many thanks and our offers for the goods you demand are as follows.

  Commodities：Voloet eye cream
  Price：100Euro, FOB Marseilles
  Quantity：200 Bottles

  Commodities：Frangrant day cream
  Price：150Euro, FOB Marseilles

Quantity: 200 Bottles

Commodities: Frangrant night cream
Price: 150Euro, FOB Marseilles
Quantity: 200 Bottles

Commodities: Votrovlet perfume
Price: 150Euro, FOB Marseilles
Quantity: 200 Bottles

Packing: Wrapped with foam plastic bag and 50 bottles in a strong wooden case.
Shipment: within 4 weeks of receiving L/C
Insurance: to be covered by the buyer
Terms of Payment: by confirmed, irrevocable L/C by draft at sight

We are offering you the most favorable price and are sure this price would be very competitive at your market.

Yours faithfully

Genei

复习情境4：还盘函（Correspondence for Counter-offers）

知识目标：1. 巩固与操练还盘函写作的要领。
2. 复习还盘函写作的常用词组、典型句式。
3. 复习还盘函写作的专业术语。
4. 复习还盘函写作的商务背景知识。

能力目标：1. 能够熟练运用本环节所复习的专业术语、常用词组、典型句式正确撰写还盘函。
2. 巩固与操练还盘函写作所需要的相关商务背景知识。

任务：风华公司收到报价后认为价格总体上是合理的，也有一定的市场竞争优势。但是由于很多中国消费者对Lancelot公司产品不是非常熟悉，需要公司对此进行一些推广宣传活动，因此致函Genei总经理，希望能得到优惠折扣。

请就此撰写一封还盘函。

要求如下：
1. 表示认为 Lancelot 公司报价总体上是合理的。
2. 说明由于需要进行一定的促销活动来进行宣传，因此要求得到 10% 的优惠折扣。

你可以借助资料库中的相关资料来撰写还盘函。

范例：

Mar. 21, 2015

Dear Mr. Genei,

Your offer of Mar. 10 has been studied carefully and we consider it reasonable in general. However, our customers are not very familiar with your products and we have to launch a series of promotions to publicize them, which means we have to reduce the service charge for a period of about six month. Therefore, we hope that you can give us a discount of 10% for the order. We are sure that you can understand this counter-offer is based on the hope of a mutually beneficial cooperation.

Please let us know your decision as soon as possible.

Yours faithfully

Lancelot

任务：Lancelot 收到了风华公司的还盘函，认为其要求的价格超过了自己的承受能力。考虑到中国市场的巨大潜力，公司决定给予对方 8% 的折扣。

请就此撰写一封还盘函。

要求如下：
1. 对风华公司未能接受己方的报价表示遗憾。
2. 强调自己产品的竞争优势。
3. 表示愿意给予风华公司 8% 的折扣。

你可以借助资料库中的相关资料来撰写还盘函。

范例：

Dear Ms. Liu,

We are very sorry to know that our offer is not accepted by your company since we believe firmly that our quote is very favorable. We are sure your customers can easily tell the huge difference between our products and those of other providers and they will be attracted by our unique quality.

However, we understand your problem and decide to give you an 8% discount which is truly unprecedented to start a successful cooperation.

Yours faithfully

Genei

复习情境5：订单函（Correspondence for Orders）

知识目标：1. 巩固与操练订单函写作的要领。
     2. 复习订单函写作的常用词组、典型句式。
     3. 复习订单函写作的专业术语。
     4. 复习订单函写作的商务背景知识。
能力目标：1. 能够熟练运用本环节所复习的专业术语、常用词组、典型句式正确撰写订单函。
     2. 巩固与操练订单函写作所需要的相关商务背景知识。

任务：收到Lancelot的报价后，风华公司认为其报价是已经可以满足公司的需求，因此决定和Lancelot开展合作，向其发出订单。
请就此撰写一封订单函。
要求如下：
品名：Voloet eye cream

案例1 从法国Lancelot公司进口化妆品

单价：每瓶 100 欧元，FOB 马赛
数量：200 瓶

品名：Frangrant day cream
单价：每瓶 150 欧元，FOB 马赛
数量：200 瓶

品名：Frangrant night cream
单价：每瓶 150 欧元，FOB 马赛
数量：200 瓶

品名：Votrovlet perfume
单价：每瓶 150 欧元，FOB 马赛
数量：200 瓶

包装：泡沫塑料包裹，50 瓶装入一木箱
交货期：收到信用证后 4 周内发货
保险：由买方投保
支付方式：不可撤销的见票即付信用证

你可以借助资料库中的相关资料来撰写订单函。

范例：

April. 10, 2015

Dear Ms. Liu,

Thank you for your offer which we consider to be reasonable and therefore, we are happy to place an initial order with you for the following：

    Commodities：Voloet eye cream
    Price：100 Euro, FOB Marseilles
    Quantity：200 Bottles

Commodities: Frangrant day cream
Price: 150 Euro, FOB Marseilles
Quantity: 200 Bottles

Commodities: Frangrant night cream
Price: 150 Euro, FOB Marseilles
Quantity: 200 Bottles

Commodities: Votrovlet perfume
Price: 150 Euro, FOB Marseilles
Quantity: 200 Bottles

Packing: Wrapped with foam plastic bag and 50 bottles in a strong wooden case
Shipment: within 4 weeks of receiving L/C
Insurance: to be covered by the buyer
Terms of Payment: by confirmed, irrevocable L/C by draft at sight

Please note that we will place bigger orders if the first order can meet our demands.

Sincerely yours

Liu Shan

复习情境6：支付方式函（Correspondence for Terms of Payment）

知识目标：1. 巩固与操练支付方式函写作的要领。
2. 复习支付方式函写作的常用词组、典型句式。
3. 复习支付方式函写作的专业术语。
4. 复习支付方式函写作的商务背景知识。

能力目标：1. 能够熟练运用本环节所复习的专业术语、常用词组、典型句式正确撰写支付方式函。
2. 巩固与操练支付方式函写作所需要的相关商务背景知识。

任务：Lancelot 公司在里昂信贷银行开立了信用证，并写信通知风华公司。
请就此撰写一封开立信用证通知函。

案例1 从法国 Lancelot 公司进口化妆品

要求如下：
1. 通知风华公司根据双方签订的编号为 FJK – 5681 的合同，L23536 – 09 号信用证已由里昂信贷银行。
2. 金额为 11 万欧元。
3. 信用证有效期截止到 2015 年 7 月 25 日。

你可以借助资料库中的相关资料来撰写开立信用证通知函。

范例：

April 25, 2015

Dear Ms. Liu Shan,

RE：Establishment of L/C under S/C No. FJK – 5681

It is our pleasure to inform you that L/C No. L23536 – 09 under the contract of FJK – 5681 has been opened with Lyon Credit Bank for Euro 110000. The L/C is valid until July 25, 2015. The above L/C will reach you very soon.

Yours faithfully

Lancelot

任务： 由于近期欧洲金融市场出现动荡，Lancelot 公司考虑到使用不可撤销的见票即付信用证成本过高，因此致函风华公司，希望将支付方式修改为即期交单。
请就此撰写一封更改支付方式请求函。
要求如下：
1. 说明请求更改支付方式的原因。
2. 请求将支付方式更改为即期交单。

你可以借助资料库中的相关资料来撰写更改支付方式请求函。

范例：

Dear Ms. Liu,

As you may have known that recently unexpected turbulence hit the European financial market, it is no more economical to pay by confirmed, irrevocable L/C. We wonder if you can agree to make amendments to the previous payment terms by replacing L/C with D/P at sight.

Your consideration of this request will be highly appreciated.

Sincerely yours

Lancelot

任务：风华公司认真研究了 Lancelot 公司更改支付方式的请求函，认为当前欧洲金融危机有逐步扩大蔓延的倾向，造成了货币市场的动荡，因此决定拒绝对方的请求。

请就此撰写一封拒绝更改支付方式的回函。

要求如下：
1. 通知对方拒绝更改原定支付方式。
2. 说明拒绝更改支付方式请求的理由。

你可以借助资料库中的相关资料来撰写回函。

范例：

Dear Mr. Genei,

We understand and feel sorry for your current problem, but our financial department believes that any payment approach other than L/C will be unacceptable to us. Therefore, we have to reject your request to make amendments in payments terms.

Yours faithfully

Liu Shan

案例1　从法国 Lancelot 公司进口化妆品

复习情境7：包装函（Correspondence for Packing）

知识目标： 1. 巩固与操练包装函写作的要领。
2. 复习包装函写作的常用词组、典型句式。
3. 复习包装函写作的专业术语。
4. 复习包装函写作的商务背景知识。

能力目标： 1. 能够熟练运用本环节所复习的专业术语、常用词组、典型句式正确撰写包装函。
2. 巩固与操练包装函写作所需要的相关商务背景知识。

任务： 由于化妆品均属于易被损坏或者污染的物品，风华公司致信 Lancelot 公司，强调严格遵循包装条款的重要性。

请就此撰写一封包装指示函。

要求如下：
1. 强调包装必须适合长途海运。
2. 要求在木箱正面标注"易碎品"的警示语。

你可以借助资料库中的相关资料来撰写包装指示函。

范例：

Dear Mr. Genei,

You may have learnt that the Chinese customers are fastidious about the product's appearance, which means perfect package is one of the essential elements in their evaluation of your products.

In order to protect the image of your product as luxurious, elegant and classic, we reiterate here that the package must be suitable for the long distance marine transportation and the directive mark of FRAGILE should be indicated on the front side of the wooden case.

We look forward to receiving your shipping advice.

Yours sincerely

Liu shan

复习情境8：保险函（Correspondence for Insurance）

知识目标： 1. 巩固与操练保险函写作的要领。
2. 复习保险函写作的常用词组、典型句式。
3. 复习保险函写作的专业术语。
4. 复习保险函写作的商务背景知识。

能力目标： 1. 能够熟练运用本环节所复习的专业术语、常用词组、典型句式正确撰写保险函。
2. 巩固与操练保险函写作所需要的相关商务背景知识。

任务： Lancelot按照合同在规定时间内安排好货运事宜，现致信风华公司，通知对方已经按照惯例为相关商品购买了保险。

请就此撰写一封告之买方购买保险的通知函。

要求如下：

1. 告知对方运输事宜已安排好，货物将由"尼尔森号"货轮承运。启运时间为8月15日，目的港为天津。
2. 告知对方已经为商品投保发票金额110%的一切险。

你可以借助资料库中的相关资料来撰写保险函。

范例：

July 10, 2015

Dear Ms. Liu,

I am glad to inform you that shipping space for the consignment has been booked on S. S. Nilsson which sails for Tianjin on August 15.

We have covered insurance on the goods against All Risks for 110% of the invoice value.

Your prompt confirmation would be appreciated.

Yours sincerely

Genei

复习情境9：运输函（Correspondence for Shipment）

知识目标：1. 巩固与操练运输函写作的要领。
2. 复习运输函写作的常用词组、典型句式。
3. 复习运输函写作的专业术语。
4. 复习运输函写作的商务背景知识。

能力目标：1. 能够熟练运用本环节所复习的专业术语、常用词组、典型句式正确撰写运输函。
2. 巩固与操练运输函写作所需要的相关商务背景知识。

任务：由于马赛港工人罢工，港口装运工作无法正常进行，"尼尔森"的起航时间也因此被推迟到9月15日。

请就此撰写一封告知对方起运时间推迟的通知函。

要求如下：

1. 告知对方起运时间推迟的原因。
2. 告知对方新的启运时间。
3. 告知对方不会逾期交货。

你可以借助资料库中的相关资料来撰写通知函。

范例：

July 20, 2015

Dear Ms. Liu,

We are very sorry to inform you that because of the workers' strike, the normal operation of Marseilles has been halted, which means the S. S. Nilsson could not leave the port until Sep. 15.

However, we can assure you that the delivery deadline will still be met

Sincerely yours

Genei

外贸运输中的"保函"

在国际海洋货物运输过程中，保函是由托运人向承运人做出的一种书面保证，以此换取承运人签发清洁提单。在国际贸易中，买方一般不愿意接受不清洁提单，银行一般也不接受不清洁提单作为议付货款的单据。因此卖方为了尽快得到清洁提单从而顺利在银行议付货款，往往会向承运人保证，如果货物残损短缺或者因为承运人签发清洁提单而引起的一切损失，都由托运人承担。

由于这种保函的出具往往造成承运人疏于对货物的检查，或者隐瞒货物真实的情况，而且托运人比较容易利用保函进行诈骗，因此在各国的法律规定及司法实践中，一般认为保函是具有欺骗性质的，因而是无效的或者是不能要求法院加以强制执行的。所以即使承运人取得了保函并由此签发了清洁提单，如果货物存在破损或灭失的情况，买方要求承运人承担运输不当的责任时，承运人不能免除责任。

但是在某些情况下，特别是因为承运人专业知识有限不了解货物的全面情况的时候，或者在承运人和托运人对货物的数量及真实情况存在分歧的时候，允许承运人通过保函进行免责。

复习情境 10：索赔和纠纷解决
(Correspondence for Claim and Settlement)

知识目标：1. 巩固与操练索赔函写作的要领。
2. 复习索赔函写作的常用词组、典型句式。
3. 复习索赔函写作的专业术语。
4. 复习索赔函写作的商务背景知识。

能力目标：1. 能够熟练运用本环节所复习的专业术语、常用词组、典型句式正确撰写索赔函。
2. 巩固与操练索赔函写作所需要的相关商务背景知识。

任务：经过漫长的等待，风华公司终于收到了 Lancelot 发出的货物。但是检验中发现 50 瓶 Voloet 眼霜破损，无法销售和使用。

案例 1 从法国 Lancelot 公司进口化妆品

请就此撰写一封索赔函。

要求如下：

1. 告知货物已收到。
2. 告知 Lancelot 50 瓶 Voloet 眼霜破损，提出索赔。

你可以借助资料库中的相关资料来撰写索赔函。

范例：

Dear Mr. Genei,

We have received your goods, but unfortunately, during the routine inspection, we were surprised to find 50 bottles of Voloet eye cream were broken, which cannot be used or sold.

We are sorry to inform you that we have to lodge a claim for the damaged goods.

Enclosed please find the quality inspection report

Yours respectfully

Liu shan

商业背景知识拓展

1. Introduction of the French Economy

France has the second largest economy in Europe and the sixth largest economy in the world. It is also considered the wealthiest European country and the world's fourth wealthiest nation in aggregate household wealth according to Credit Suisse's Global Wealth Report.

The cornerstone for France's economy is the chemical industry, which serves as the springboard for many of its other manufacturing activities. Tourism is also a large part of the French economy, as France is one of the most popular and iconic tourist destination in the world. France is the home for many Fortune Global 500 enterprises, which also ranked France fourth, behind the USA, China, and Japan, for global economic importance. Paris has the second largest number of Fortune Global 500 company corporate headquarters of any city in the world.

Focused primarily on private ownership with little government intervention, the government, however, does play a significant role in the French economy. In 2014, government spending made up 56 percent of GDP. Moreover, France has some of the highest government standards for labor, including hours and wages, of any European nation. The government also owns shares in a number of corporations in key sectors, including banking, energy production and distribution, automobiles, transportation, and telecommunications.

2. France and China: Free and Friendly Trade

France and China have agreed to a Free Trade Agreement after ten years of negotiations. This is the third major FTA between France and a major Asian economy this year, the other two being Japan and Republic of Korea. The Coalition is, of course, proud of its efforts.

Great friendship between two nations planning on making each other even richer was the exuberant tone of most politicians discussing the deal. All previous skepticism regarding China and its investment into France is forgotten by Coalition politicians, who had to explain it to the media as details will not fully be released until next year, after it is formally signed.

Obviously, the government deserves a pat on the back. And why not, as most have pointed out that France should do very well out of the deal. Tariffs on French wine will disappear over four years, which is currently 14 to 30 percent. China imported some 9 billion Euro worth of French agricultural goods last year. The resources sector will benefit, with the removal of tariffs on all energy products and on pharmaceuticals over four years. The services sector is also expected to do well: tourism, education and elderly care services from France can now more easily be set up in China. Ultimately 95 percent of French exports to China will be tariff free within the next decade or so.

There has been no agreement on a deal for certain agricultural products such as rice, wheat, sugar, cotton and oilseed. China is now allowed to send its skilled labor to France to work, which has prompted some inevitable angst. The French Trade Minister has to reassure critics it would not be at the expense of French jobs, though critics have pointed to China's history of sending its workers to Africa and Asia. The government will screen all state-owned enterprise investment. Chinese SOE investment in France has been a concern for some time given allegations of corruption and their opaque nature. Private Chinese business will not face such hurdles. Property purchases will not be under any especial review or scrutiny despite ongoing and very public concerns over Chinese purchases of much French property that have, some critics allege, verged on xenophobic in their worries of rich Chinese forcing up the market.

案例 2 从加拿大 Bernstein 公司进口木材

商业背景设定：

进口商：精工家具公司（Jinggong Furniture），中国最大的实木家具生产企业，致力于生产和销售各种高档实木家具。

公司地址：中国江苏省常州市解放路 15 号
总经理：张华民
主要产品：高档实木家具

进口商：Bernstein，加拿大最大的木材开采和初加工公司，其生产的黑胡桃木、红橡木等高档木材在国际家具市场享有盛誉，是很多高档家具制造公司的首选合作伙伴。

公司地址：639 Lincoln Street，Montreal，Canada
董事长：Robert Bernstein

精工家具公司根据中国实木家具市场的新变化，设计研发了一系列针对高端客户的美式家具，需要大批高档黑胡桃木材料。公司通过市场调查发现中国客户对产于加拿大的北美黑胡桃情有独钟，因此与 Bernstein 公司联系，希望能从该公司进口木材。

巩固情境 1：建交函
(Correspondence for Establishing Business Relations)

知识目标：1. 复习与操练建交函写作的要领。
    2. 巩固建交函写作的常用词组、典型句式。
    3. 巩固建交函写作的专业术语。
    4. 巩固建交函写作的商务背景知识。
能力目标：1. 能够熟练运用本环节所巩固的专业术语、常用词组、典型句式正确撰写建交函。
    2. 掌握建交函写作所需要的相关商务背景知识。

任务： 精工家具公司总经理张华民致信 Bernstein 公司董事长伯恩斯坦先生，说明公司基本情况，表达了与对方合作的意愿，希望早日得到回复。

请就此撰写一封建交函。
要求如下：
1. 介绍本公司基本情况。
2. 表达合作意愿。

你可以借助资料库中的相关资料来撰写建交函。

范例：

Jinggong Furniture
No. 15 Jiefang Road,
Changzhou, Jiangsu
P. R. China
Jan. 20, 2015

Bernstein
639 Lincoln Street
Montreal
Canada

Dear Mr. Bernstein,

Your company has been recommended to us by our business partners as a high quality and trustworthy wood producer.

Our company is a Chinese maker of luxurious pure wood furniture and enjoys great popularity among high-end customers, for whom we have developed a series of North American style furniture. Our market study demonstrates that the black walnut timber is the top 1 choice for many Chinese customers and we are writing to you in hope of entering into a mutual beneficial relationship with your company. The Chinese timber market is growing swiftly and attracting more and more foreign wood producers. We believe our company is the best partner for any timber company who wants to enter this market.

Your prompt and favorable reply will be highly appreciated.

Sincerely yours

Zhang Huamin

General Manager

　　任务： Bernstein 正有意进入蓬勃发展的中国木材市场，因此非常重视精工家具公司的来函，对此进行了认真的研究。公司高级管理层达成了一致意见，即精工家具公司是 Bernstein 进入中国市场的最佳合作伙伴，因此决定和精工家具公司就产品的销售问题进行协商。伯恩斯坦先生代表公司给张华民总经理回函，表示愿意开展合作。
　　请就此撰写一封回函。
　　要求如下：
　　1. 感谢对方来函。
　　2. 希望精工公司能告知所需木材的详细要求。

你可以借助资料库中的相关资料来撰写询盘函。

范例：

Dear Mr. Zhang,

Your letter has been received with many thanks. We believe that the Chinese timber market is very important for the future development of Bernstein and we feel honored to have this opportunity to cooperate with a company like yours.

We wonder if you could send us your requisitions in detail, so we can arrange for the further communication.

Thank you again.

Sincerely yours

案例2　从加拿大 Bernstein 公司进口木材

Robert Bernstein

President

巩固情境2：询盘函（Correspondence for Enquiry）

知识目标： 1. 复习与操练询盘函写作的要领。
2. 巩固询盘函的常用词组、典型句式。
3. 巩固询盘函写作的专业术语。
4. 巩固询盘函写作的商务背景知识。

能力目标： 1. 能够熟练运用本环节所巩固的专业术语、常用词组、典型句式正确撰写询盘函。
2. 掌握询盘函写作所需要的相关商务背景知识。

任务： 精工家具公司很高兴能与Bernstein建立联系，由于即将进入家具生产和销售的旺季，因此立刻致函，要求对方寄送木材样品以供测试和检验。

请就此撰写一封询盘函。

要求如下：

1. 感谢对方来函。
2. 要求尽快寄送规格为8－11″的黑胡桃木板5块以供测试使用。

你可以借助资料库中的相关资料来撰写询盘函。

范例：

Dear Mr. Bernstein,

Your letter has been received with many thanks and your sincerity is very impressive. As the high season is coming, we hope you could send us for test 5 8－11″ black walnut boards. If the samples can meet our specific demands for the new series, we will place an order with you immediately.

Best regards.

Sincerely yours

Zhang Huamin

　　任务：Bernstein 公司收信后迅速给精工家具公司寄送了所要求的样品。精工公司经过测试，认为其质地、颜色、油性等指标均达到了公司的要求，因此决定立刻向 Bernstein 公司订购产品。张华民总经理致函伯恩斯坦先生，告知对方计划首批购买 50 万板尺的黑胡桃木，要求对方进行报价。

　　请就此撰写一封要求报价的询盘函。

　　要求如下：

　　1. 对寄送样品表示满意。

　　2. 告知对方计划订购 50 万板尺。

　　3. 请求 Bernstein 对此进行 CIF 上海报价。

你可以借助资料库中的相关资料来撰写询盘函。

范例：

Feb. 20, 2015

Dear Mr. Bernstein,

We have received your samples and they passed our test very successfully. We hereby ask you to quote us the most favorable CIF Shanghai for 500 TBF of your black walnut timber. Please give us the details of your price and terms of payment.

Your prompt reply is appreciated.

Sincerely yours

Zhang Huamin

巩固情境 3：发盘函（Correspondence for Offers）

　　知识目标：1. 复习与操练发盘函写作的要领。

2. 巩固发盘函写作的常用词组、典型句式。
3. 巩固发盘函写作的专业术语。
4. 巩固发盘函写作的商务背景知识。

能力目标： 1. 能够熟练运用本环节所巩固的专业术语、常用词组、典型句式正确撰写发盘函。
2. 掌握发盘函写作所需要的相关商务背景知识。

任务： Bernstein 收到精工家具的询盘函，很快就对其进行了发盘。
请就此撰写一封发盘函。
要求如下：
品名：黑胡桃木材
单价：每千板尺 1000 美元，CIF 上海
数量：50 万板尺
交货期：收到信用证后 4 周内发货
保险：由卖方投保
支付方式：不可撤销的见票即付信用证
此发盘有效期为 7 天

你可以借助资料库中的相关资料来撰写发盘函。

范例：

Dear Mr. Zhang,

We are very happy to hear from you and excited about having this opportunity to cooperate with you. Our offers for the timber are as follows.

    Commodity：Black Walnut Timber
    Price：US $ 1000/TBF, CIF Shanghai
    Quantity：500 TBF tons
    Shipment：within 4 weeks of receiving L/C
    Insurance：to be covered by the buyer
    Terms of Payment：by irrevocable L/C by draft at sight

This is a very favorable and competitive price which is valid for 7 days. So please inform us your decision asap.

Yours faithfully

Robert Bernstein

巩固情境4：还盘函（Correspondence for Counter-offers）

知识目标：1. 复习与操练还盘函写作的要领。
2. 巩固还盘函写作的常用词组、典型句式。
3. 巩固还盘函写作的专业术语。
4. 巩固还盘函写作的商务背景知识。

能力目标：1. 能够熟练运用本环节所巩固的专业术语、常用词组、典型句式正确撰写还盘函。
2. 掌握还盘函写作所需要的相关商务背景知识。

任务：精工家具公司收到Bernstein的报价后，认为价格有些偏高，希望能得到20%优惠折扣。Bernstein认为对方的还价超过了公司的承受能力，拒绝了精工公司的请求。但是承诺在今后的交易中会给予精工公司最优先的木材选择权。

请就此撰写一封还盘函。
要求如下：
1. 拒绝精工公司的还价，对此表示遗憾。
2. 强调自己产品的竞争优势。
3. 表示今后会给予精工公司最优先的木材选择权。

你可以借助资料库中的相关资料来撰写还盘函。

范例：

Dear Mr. Zhang,

We are very sorry to inform you that after serious consideration and study, we found your request of 20% discount is beyond our capacity. The price we quoted is very favorable, especially considering the current soaring market for the best quality timber.

案例2 从加拿大Bernstein公司进口木材

We will grand you the first priority for the best quality timber in the future if this deal succeeds.

Yours faithfully

Robert Bernstein

巩固情境 5：订单函（Correspondence for Orders）

知识目标：1. 复习与操练订单函写作的要领。
2. 巩固订单函写作的常用词组、典型句式。
3. 巩固订单函写作的专业术语。
4. 巩固订单函写作的商务背景知识。

能力目标：1. 能够熟练运用本环节所巩固的专业术语、常用词组、典型句式正确撰写订单函。
2. 掌握订单函写作所需要的相关商务背景知识。

任务：精工家具公司重新进行了市场调研，认为 Bernstein 公司产品价格虽然高于公司预期，但是考虑到木材市场价格上升趋势明显，其产品的性价比仍然具有相当的优势，因此决定向其购买 50 万板尺黑胡桃木。

请就此撰写一封订单函。

要求如下：
1. 订购购买 50 万板尺黑胡桃木。
2. 每千板尺 1000 美元，CIF 上海。
3. 收到信用证后 4 周内发货。
4. 保险由卖方投保。
5. 支付方式为不可撤销的见票即付信用证。
6. 强调货品品质须与样品一致。

你可以借助资料库中的相关资料来撰写订单函。

范例：

Dear Mr. Zhang,

After considering your offers, especially in the view of future cooperation, we made the decision to place an initial order with you for the following:

    Commodity: Black Walnut Timber
    Price: US＄1000/TBF, CIF Shanghai
    Quantity: 500 TBF
    Shipment: within 4 weeks of receiving L/C
    Insurance: to be covered by the buyer
    Terms of Payment: by irrevocable L/C by draft at sight

Please note that the quality of your delivery should be strictly in accordance with that of the samples. Continuous and bigger orders will definitely follow if the first deal is successful.

Sincerely yours

Zhang Huamin

巩固情境6：支付方式函（Correspondence for Terms of Payment）

知识目标：1. 复习与操练支付方式函写作的要领。
            2. 巩固支付方式函写作的常用词组、典型句式。
            3. 巩固支付方式函写作的专业术语。
            4. 巩固支付方式函写作的商务背景知识。
能力目标：1. 能够熟练运用本环节所巩固的专业术语、常用词组、典型句式正确撰写支付方式函。
            2. 掌握支付方式函写作所需要的相关商务背景知识。

任务：精工家具公司按照合同要求按期在银行开立了信用证，并写信通知Bernstein。请就此撰写一封开立信用证通知函。
要求如下：
1. 通知Bernstein已由加拿大枫叶银行开立了编号为TGF29005的信用证。
2. 金额为500000美元。
3. 信用证有效期为2016年10月30日。

你可以借助资料库中的相关资料来撰写开立信用证通知函。

范例：

Dear Mr. Bernstein,

I am writing to tell you that we have opened L/C No. TGF29005 with Maple Leave Bank of Canada for 500000US dollars. The L/C is valid until 30th October, 2016. The L/C will be sent to you promptly.

Yours faithfully

Zhang Huamin

常用付款方式的风险分析：

D/P（document against payment）：付款交单，可分为即期交单（D/P at Sight）和远期交单（D/P after sight or after date）。它实质上是一种托收方式，出口方的交单以进口方的付款为前提，即进口方付款后才能向代收银行领取单据。由于没有第三方担保，也没有定金，这种付款方式相对 L/C 而言有一定风险。如果进口商拒收货物，不到银行赎单，银行会将单据退回，出口方的货物另行处理，这往往会造成较大的损失。因此只有客户信誉较好或者是双方有长期合作的关系时才会适度使用。

巩固情境7：包装函（Correspondence for Packing）

知识目标：1. 复习与操练包装函写作的要领。
2. 巩固包装函写作的常用词组、典型句式。
3. 巩固包装函写作的专业术语。
4. 巩固包装函写作的商务背景知识。

能力目标：1. 能够熟练运用本环节所巩固的专业术语、常用词组、典型句式正确撰写包装函。
2. 掌握包装函写作所需要的相关商务背景知识。

任务：由于木材产品在装卸、运输途中易于损害，尤其是要海运，过程漫长，容易受到潮湿损害，因此致函 Bernstein，要求其加强对产品包装工作的管理，强调务必按照要求对产品进行认真的包装。

请就此撰写一封包装指示函。

要求如下：
1. 强调长途海运对于包装提出了较高的要求。
2. 要求用防水布包裹。
3. 要求标注"保持干燥"的警示语。

你可以借助资料库中的相关资料来撰写包装指示函。

范例：

Dear Mr. Bernstein,

As you may be aware of the hazards of marine transportation, especially water damage, we hereby stress the importance of proper packing.

Taking in consideration of long distance and unpredictable weather, we strongly request you to cover the timber with waterproof cloth. Furthermore, indicative mark of KEEP DRY should be shown clearly.

Best regards

Yours sincerely

Zhang Huamin

巩固情境8：保险函（Correspondence for Insurance）

知识目标：1. 复习与操练保险函写作的要领。
2. 巩固保险函写作的常用词组、典型句式。
3. 巩固保险函写作的专业术语。
4. 巩固保险函写作的商务背景知识。

能力目标：1. 能够熟练运用本环节所巩固的专业术语、常用词组、典型句式正确撰写保险函。

案例2　从加拿大 Bernstein 公司进口木材

2. 掌握保险函写作所需要的相关商务背景知识。

任务：Bernstein 公司按照合同在规定时间内安排好货运事宜，现致信精工家具，告知对方已为相关商品购买保险。

请就此撰写一封要求买方购买保险的通知函。

要求如下：

1. 告知对方已安排好运输事宜，货物将由"威尔逊号"货轮承运。启运时间为 8 月 15 日。

2. 告知对方为商品投保了平安险、水渍险和附加险。

你可以借助资料库中的相关资料来撰写保险函。

范例：

Dear Mr. Zhang,

We hereby inform you that shipping space for the consignment has been booked on S. S. Wilson which sails on August 15 and we have arranged insurances covering F. P. A, W. P. A and Extraneous Risks.

If you have any further instructions, please do not hesitate to inform us.

Yours sincerely

Robert Bernstein

巩固情境 9：运输函（Correspondence for Shipment）

知识目标：1. 复习与操练运输函写作的要领。
2. 巩固运输函写作的常用词组、典型句式。
3. 巩固运输函写作的专业术语。
4. 巩固运输函写作的商务背景知识。

能力目标：1. 能够熟练运用本环节所巩固的专业术语、常用词组、典型句式正确撰写运输函。
2. 掌握运输函写作所需要的相关商务背景知识。

任务：由于市场竞争加剧，精工家具发现高端市场上开始出现了与自己设计相似的产品。为了尽快推出新产品，占领市场，精工家具公司希望对方可以提前完成货品的装运，将起航时间尽可能地提前。

请就此撰写一封请求对方起运时间提前的通知函。

要求如下：
1. 告知对方请求起运时间提前的原因。
2. 告知对方愿意承担这一改变所发生的合理费用。

你可以借助资料库中的相关资料来撰写通知函。

范例：

July 20, 2015

Dear Mr. Bernstein,

To our surprise, we find there are more and more furniture on the market which is similar to our design. Therefore, we hereby ask you to do us a favor and finish the loading a.s.a.p., so that we can have more time to gain back the market share. Any reasonable expenses generated by this requirement would be at our side.

Your prompt consideration and favorable reply will be highly appreciated.

Sincerely yours

Zhang Huamin

巩固情境 10：索赔和纠纷解决
(Correspondence for Claim and Settlement)

知识目标：1. 复习与操练索赔函写作的要领。
　　　　　2. 巩固索赔函写作的常用词组、典型句式。
　　　　　3. 巩固索赔函写作的专业术语。

案例 2　从加拿大 Bernstein 公司进口木材

4. 巩固索赔函写作的商务背景知识。

能力目标： 1. 能够熟练运用本环节所巩固的专业术语、常用词组、典型句式正确撰写索赔函。

2. 掌握索赔函写作所需要的相关商务背景知识。

任务： 精工家具公司终于收到了货物，但是在验收时发现有近 10000 板尺的木材被海水浸泡，严重影响了外观和质地。

请就此撰写一封索赔函。

要求如下：

1. 告知 Bernstein 公司货物已收到。
2. 告知对方有近 10000 板尺木材发生水浸，提出索赔。

你可以借助资料库中的相关资料来撰写索赔函。

范例：

Dear Mr. Bernstein,

We have received the timber ordered, but regret to inform you that nearly 10 TBF of the wood was contaminated by the sea water, which seriously damaged the timbers appearance as well as the texture. We are sorry to inform you that we have to lodge a claim.

We should be grateful if you let us promptly have your opinions about these requirements.

Yours respectfully

Zhang Huamin

牢记提单的四个特点，轻松搞定运输环节

什么是提单？它是货物装船后或承运人收到货物后，由船长或承运人的代理人签发，证明收到提单上所载明的货物，允诺将货物运至指定的目的地并将货物交付给收货人的凭证。提单是国际贸易中的重要文件，通常具有以下四个特点：

（1）提单只是货物运输合同的证据之一。由于提单上只有一方当事人代表的签字，而不是由双方当事人共同签字，在形式上不符合合同的要求，因此很多国家不承认提单是承运人与托运人之间的运输合同，而是作为二者订立的运输合同的证据。

（2）提单是承运人对货物出具的收据。承运人签发提单就表示其已经收到了提单上所载明的货物，货物在交付给承运人时的状况以提单的标注为准。如果承运人没有收到货物，或者货物与提单上的记载不符，但是由于种种原因签发了提单，并且没有对收到的货物进行任何批注，那么在买方收到货物的时候，就完全有理由认为货物在装运前是完好无损、符合合同要求的。如果买方发现货物出现了破损或灭失，就可以将其视为运输过程中发生的并有权要求承运人承担责任。

（3）提单是一种物权凭证。按照商业惯例，占有提单就相当于占有货物，而提单的转让通常具有与交货本身同样的效果。因此，提单是货物占有权的凭证。由于提单具有这种物权凭证的作用，在国际贸易中，它可以作为买卖的标的物和向银行押汇的担保物。

（4）提单有多种类型。作为一种国际贸易单据，提单可以根据不同的标准进行分类。例如按照签发时间是在货物装船之前还是在装船之后，可以将其分为已装船提单或备运提单；按照承运人对货物的外表状态有无加列批注，可以分为清洁提单和不清洁提单；按照提单的收货人抬头的分类，可以分为记名提单、不记名提单和指示提单；按照运输方式分类，可以分为直达提单和海上联运提单；按照经营运输方式的不同，可以分为班轮提单或租船合同项下的提单等等。

商业背景知识拓展

1. The Introduction of Canadian Economy

Being the 11th largest world economy, Canada is one of the world's wealthiest nations and a member of the Organization for Economic Co-operation and Development (OECD) and Group of Seven (G7).

The Canadian economic system has elements of private and public enterprise. Canada has a private to public property ownership ratio of 60 : 40 and one of the highest levels of economic freedom in the world. Canada's economy closely resembles the United States in its market-oriented economic system and pattern of production. Canadian economy is dominated by the service sector, which employs about 75 percent of the nation's population.

Canada is unique among developed nations due to the importance of its primary sector, with logging and oil being two of Canada's most important industries. Canada also has a sizable manufacturing sector based on the automobile and aircraft industry. Canada has the eighth largest commercial fishing and seafood industry in the world and a well-developed technology sector that includes a world-leading entertainment software industry. International trade in Canada's natural resources makes up a large part of its economy. In 2009, agricultural, energy, forestry and mining exports made up 58 percent of Canada's total exports. Machinery, equipment, automotive products and other manufactured goods made up 38 percent of exports that year. America is Canada's largest trading partner, accounting for 73 percent of exports and 63 percent of imports.

As the country devotes more resources to the modern industry, primary products are slowly becoming less important to the Canadian economy. The primary industries only employ about 4 percent of Canadian and account for just 6.2 percent of GDP. Nevertheless, Canada still remains a world leader in the production of many natural resources such as gold, nickel, uranium, diamonds, lead, and crude petroleum.

2. Sino-Canadian Economic Cooperation

In recent years, the bilateral trade and economic cooperation between China and Canada has been developing steadily and made great achievements. Investment cooperation between the two countries develops fast. Canada has become one of the most important overseas investment destinations for China, and the bilateral investment cooperation is more and more pluralistic. In 2011, China-Canada trade increased by 27.8% year on year; and that is expected to reach US $50 billion in 2012.

At present, Sino-Canadian bilateral trade accounts for merely 1.3% of China's total foreign trade and 5.2% of Canada's total; the bilateral direct investment only makes up 1% of their respective attracted FDI, which does not match the economic strength of the two nations and shows huge development potential.

Against the increasing downturn of global economy, China and Canada's further deepening bilateral trade and economic cooperation. Many experts, therefore, are calling on a closer trade and economic cooperation. The two countries are strengthening cooperation mechanisms to create better conditions for trade between enterprises of the two sides. They aim to promote the achievements of the economic complementarities study to transform into concrete steps for advancing bilateral trade and economic cooperation, so as to boost the in-depth development of bilateral trade and investment. China expects to expand import from Canada, and promote the balanced development of the bilateral trade. It is expected that more Canadian enterprises will invest in China.

The overall China-Canada cooperation level is also enhanced by provincial and municipal cooperation, which encourages provinces and municipals of the two nations to form a multi-tiered and all-round pattern for cooperation and development as soon as possible; and guide enterprises of the two sides to reinforce cooperation in energy resources, energy conservation and environmental protection, information technology, aerospace, automobiles and auto parts, agriculture and fishery, infrastructure, etc.

案例3　从韩国佑赫会社进口液晶显示屏

商业背景设定：

进口商：华通显示器（Huatong Displayer Co.），中国知名的显示器制造企业，其产品在世界多国广受欢迎。目前公司正在升级产品系列，研发出一款新式显示器，需要配用对比度较高的液晶显示屏。

总经理：刘振亚

主要产品：高档显示器

进口商：Yuhe Firm，佑赫会社是韩国最大的液晶面板制造商之一，其刚研发制造的TVG-235型液晶显示屏的各项技术指标均达到了世界领先水平。

销售部经理：金永中（Kim Yun-Jung）

随着普通液晶显示器市场的饱和，各生产厂商之间的竞争日趋激烈。华通显示器公司敏锐地认识到了这个问题，将高清晰度产品设定为公司新的利润增长点。华通针对市场的需求，开发出一款高清晰度液晶显示器。华通显示器公司认为佑赫会社的产品符合其产品各项指标的要求，因此与佑赫会社取得联系，希望能和对方建立起良好的合作关系。

学习情境1：建交函
(Correspondence for Establishing Business Relations)

知识目标： 1. 复习与操练建交函写作的要领。
2. 巩固建交函写作的常用词组、典型句式。
3. 巩固建交函写作的专业术语。
4. 巩固建交函写作的商务背景知识。

能力目标： 1. 能够熟练运用本环节所巩固的专业术语、常用词组、典型句式正确撰写建交函。
2. 复习操练建交函写作所需要的相关商务背景知识。

任务： 华通显示器公司总经理刘振亚给佑赫会社总经理金永中先生发出一封建交函，表达与对方合作的意愿，并且希望早日得到回复。

请就此撰写一封建交函。

要求如下：

1. 介绍本公司基本情况。
2. 表达合作意愿。

你可以借助资料库中的相关资料来撰写建交函。

范例：

Dear Mr. Kim,

Your firm has been recommended to us by the Commercial Counselor's Office of South Korea in Shanghai, and we understand that you are a leading producer of high resolution LED screen.

As one of the biggest manufacturers of LED displayer, our product is very popular on various countries' market. We are launching a newest model and your TVG-235 screen is considered the best material for our new product.

We hope that we can cooperate which we believe will be mutually beneficial. You requirements of further details about our product will be satisfied with great enthusiasm.

We are looking forward to hearing from you soon.

Sincerely yours

Liu Zhenya

General Manager

巩固情境2：询盘函（Correspondence for Enquiry）

知识目标：1. 复习与操练询盘函写作的要领。
2. 巩固询盘函的常用词组、典型句式。
3. 巩固询盘函写作的专业术语。
4. 巩固询盘函写作的商务背景知识。

能力目标：1. 能够熟练运用本环节所巩固的专业术语、常用词组、典型句式正确撰写询盘函。
2. 复习操练询盘函写作所需要的相关商务背景知识。

任务：佑赫会社收到了华通显示器公司建立贸易关系的来函，认为中国市场成长迅速，加强与中国生产商的合作有助于公司进一步扩大市场占有率，因此决定和华通显示器公司合作。华通公司对其寄送的样品进行了测试，结果表明佑赫会社的产品完全满足华通公司的要求，因此决定订购1000台TVG－235型液晶显示屏，要求对方进行报价。
请就此撰写一封要求报价的询盘函。
要求如下：
1. 对寄送样品表示满意，表示要订购1000台的TVG－235显示屏。
2. 请求对此进行报价。

你可以借助资料库中的相关资料来撰写询盘函

范例：

Dear Mr. Kim,

We are writing to inform you that your samples have been passed our test successfully, which proves it can match our newest product perfectly. We ask you to quote us the lowest CIF Zhanjiang for 1000 units of your TVG－235 screen.

If your price is reasonable, more orders will follow.

Your early replies will be welcomed.

Sincerely yours

Liu Zhenya

巩固情境3：发盘函（Correspondence for Offers）

知识目标：1. 复习与操练发盘函写作的要领。

2. 巩固发盘函写作的常用词组、典型句式。
3. 巩固发盘函写作的专业术语。
4. 巩固发盘函写作的商务背景知识。

能力目标： 1. 能够熟练运用本环节所巩固的专业术语、常用词组、典型句式正确撰写发盘函。
2. 复习操练发盘函写作所需要的相关商务背景知识。

任务： 佑赫会社收到询盘函后，很快就向华通公司进行了发盘。
请就此撰写一封发盘函。
要求如下：
品名：TVG-235 液晶面板
单价：每台 100 美元，CIF 湛江
数量：1000 台
包装：木板箱，每箱 100 台
交货期：收到信用证后 4 周内发货
支付方式：保兑的、不可撤销见票即付信用证
发盘有效期为 3 周

你可以借助资料库中的相关资料来撰写发盘函。

范例：

Dear Mr. Liu,

Your enquiry has been received and our offers are as follows.

    Commodity：TVG-235 LED Screen
    Price：US $ 100 per unit, CIF Zhanjiang
    Quantity：1000 uints
    Packing：100 units in a wooden box
    Delivery：within 4 weeks of receiving L/C
    Term of Payment：by confirmed, irrevocable L/C at sight

We believe this price would be very competitive at your market. Our offer will be revoked if not accepted within 3 weeks.

Your early decision would be appreciated.

Yours faithfully

Kim Yun-jung

不同付款方式的注意要点：
（1）无论新老客户、不管成交量大小，首选以 L/C 方式为主要付款条件来签合同。对其他条款也要认真审核，如不能做到，要及时通知客户修改；认真检查审核单据，做到单单相符、单证相符，不给不法商人以任何可乘之机。

（2）T/T、D/A、D/P 付款是以商业信誉为担保的付款方式，公司必须全面彻底了解客户，必要时应该通过有关驻外机构进行资信调查。在没有搞清楚客户全部情况前不能贸然接受 T/T、D/P 付款。

（3）加强对合同和信用证的管理。公司不能放松对业务的管理和监督，如无特殊原因，必须采用 L/C 付款。对于 D/A、D/P、M/T 下成交的，必须规定权限范围；无论何种付款方式都要及时查款。T/T 项下没有收到货款，不能寄 B/L。

（4）加强与银行的业务沟通，自觉接受银行的指导。无论 L/C 还是 D/P、D/A 业务，外贸公司必须与银行保持密切合作，接受银行指导和业务培训，提高公司结汇水平。

巩固情境 4：还盘函（Correspondence for Counter-offers）

知识目标：1. 复习与操练还盘函写作的要领。
2. 巩固还盘函写作的常用词组、典型句式。
3. 巩固还盘函写作的专业术语。
4. 巩固还盘函写作的商务背景知识。

能力目标：1. 能够熟练运用本环节所巩固的专业术语、常用词组、典型句式正确撰写还盘函。
2. 复习操练还盘函写作所需要的相关商务背景知识。

任务：华通显示器公司收到佑赫会社的报价后，认为这个价格偏高，不利于其产品的推广，因此致函希望能得到更加优惠的价格。

请就此撰写一封还盘函。

要求如下：

1. 告知佑赫会社其报价偏高。

2. 说明这一价格将严重损害产品的竞争力。
3. 希望单价能够降到80美元。

你可以借助资料库中的相关资料来撰写还盘函。

范例：

Dear Mr. Kim,

We have received and seriously studied your quote, which we found with regret to be too high. This price will substantially increase the cost of our product and damage its competitiveness on the market.

We wonder if you can lower your price to $80 each piece, a reasonable price that we can accept.

We are anticipating your favorable reply.

Yours faithfully

Liu Zhenya

巩固情境5：订单函（Correspondence for Orders）

知识目标：1. 复习与操练订单函写作的要领。
2. 巩固订单函写作的常用词组、典型句式。
3. 巩固订单函写作的专业术语。
4. 巩固订单函写作的商务背景知识。

能力目标：1. 能够熟练运用本环节所巩固的专业术语、常用词组、典型句式正确撰写订单函。
2. 复习操练订单函写作所需要的相关商务背景知识。

任务：经过双方的多次协商谈判，最终将价格确定为每台80美元，华通公司发出了1000台显示屏的订单。

请就此撰写一封订单函。
要求如下：
1. 订购1000台TVG-235液晶显示屏
2. 每台80美元，CIF湛江价
3. 木板箱，每箱100台
4. 收到信用证后4周内发货
5. 支付方式为不可撤销的即期信用证

你可以借助资料库中的相关资料来撰写订单函。

范例：

Dear Mr. Kim,

Considering your offers comprehensively and in view of the long term cooperation, we finally decide to place an initial order with you for the following:

> Commodity：TVG-235 LED
> Price：US＄80 per unit, CIF Zhanjiang
> Quantity：1000 units
> Packing：100 units in a wooden box
> Delivery：within 4 weeks of receiving L/C
> Term of Payment：by confirmed, irrevocable L/C at sight

Please make sure the quality of the merchandise is in strict accordance with the samples and we believe the success of this initial order will lead to bigger deals between us.

Sincerely yours

Liu Zhenya

巩固情境6：支付方式函（Correspondence for Term of Payment）

知识目标：1. 复习与操练支付方式函写作的要领。

2. 巩固支付方式函写作的常用词组、典型句式。
3. 巩固支付方式函写作的专业术语。
4. 巩固支付方式函写作的商务背景知识。

能力目标：1. 能够熟练运用本环节所巩固的专业术语、常用词组、典型句式正确撰写支付方式函。
2. 复习操练支付方式函写作所需要的相关商务背景知识。

任务：佑赫会社按照合同要求按期在银行开立了信用证，并通知华通显示器公司。
请就此撰写一封开立信用证通知函。
要求如下：
1. 通知华通显示器公司佑赫会社已经在韩国三星银行开立了编号为 35421 的以华通显示器公司为受益人的不可撤销的跟单信用证。
2. 金额为 80000 美元。
3. 信用证有效期为 2015 年 10 月 20 日。

你可以借助资料库中的相关资料来撰写开立信用证通知函。

范例：

Dear Mr. Liu Zhenya,

We have instructed the Samsung Bank of South Korea to open an irrevocable documentary letter of credit No. 35421 in your favor. The amount is US $ 80000 and is valid until 20th October, 2015. The L/C will be sent to you very soon.

Yours faithfully

Kim Yun-Jung

巩固情境7：包装函（Correspondence for Packing）

知识目标：1. 复习与操练包装函写作的要领。
2. 巩固包装函写作的常用词组、典型句式。
3. 巩固包装函写作的专业术语。
4. 巩固包装函写作的商务背景知识。

能力目标： 1. 能够熟练运用本环节所巩固的专业术语、常用词组、典型句式正确撰写包装函。
2. 复习操练包装函写作所需要的相关商务背景知识。

任务： 华通显示器公司致函佑赫会社，明确包装相关的条款和包装要求，强调务必按照要求对产品进行认真的包装。

请就此撰写一封包装指示函。

要求如下：
1. 强调包装必须符合长途海运的要求。
2. 要求将显示屏用防水纸包裹后放置在木箱中，每100台板一箱。
3. 强调防潮、防震。

你可以借助资料库中的相关资料来撰写包装指示函。

范例：

Jun. 20, 2015

Dear Mr. Kim,

To avoid any problems caused by poor packaging, we think it is necessary to reiterate the following instructions:

    1. The packing should be seaworthy and suitable for long distance marine transportation.
    2. The screens should be wrapped with waterproof paper before being placed in the wooden case and every wooden case should contain 100 units.
    3. The goods must be well protected against moisture and shock.

We look forward to hearing from you.

Yours sincerely,

Liu Zhenya

巩固情境 8：保险函（Correspondence for Insurance）

知识目标： 1. 复习与操练保险函写作的要领。
2. 巩固保险函写作的常用词组、典型句式。
3. 巩固保险函写作的专业术语。
4. 巩固保险函写作的商务背景知识。

能力目标： 1. 能够熟练运用本环节所巩固的专业术语、常用词组、典型句式正确撰写保险函。
2. 复习操练保险函写作所需要的相关商务背景知识。

任务： 在货物即将启运前，华通显示器公司致信佑赫会社，要求其为相关货物增加附加险。

请就此撰写一封要求卖方代为购买保险的请求函。

要求如下：

1. 请求华通按发票金额的 50% 代为购买附加险。
2. 承诺收到账单后会立即付还佑赫会社所垫付的保费。

你可以借助资料库中的相关资料来撰写保险函。

范例：

Dear Mr. Kim,

We are sorry to raise this issue so late, but still hope you manage to buy insurance covering Extraneous Risks 50% of the invoice value. We shall refund the premium immediately upon receipt of your debit note.

Your approval would be highly appreciated.

Yours sincerely

Liu Zhenya

巩固情境 9：索赔和纠纷解决
(Correspondence for Claim and Settlement)

知识目标：1. 复习与操练索赔函写作的要领。
2. 巩固索赔函写作的常用词组、典型句式。
3. 巩固索赔函写作的专业术语。
4. 巩固索赔函写作的商务背景知识。

能力目标：1. 能够熟练运用本环节所巩固的专业术语、常用词组、典型句式正确撰写索赔函。
2. 复习操练索赔函写作所需要的相关商务背景知识。

任务：经过一个多月的长途海运后，华通公司订购的显示器终于顺利抵达湛江港。但是验收货物时，发现有一个木箱内的显示器并非合同中规定的 TVG-235 型，因此提出索赔。请就此撰写一封索赔函。

要求如下：
1. 告知佑赫会社货物已收到。
2. 告知对方有一箱显示器并非订购的型号，因此要求赔偿 10 万美元。

你可以借助资料库中的相关资料来撰写索赔函。

范例：

Dear Mr. Kim,

The ordered goods have reached our port, but we found that the screens in one wooden case are not the TVG-235 type as stipulated in our sales contract.

We are very sorry to inform you that we have to ask you a compensation of US $ 100000.

Yours respectfully

Liu Zhenya

商业背景知识拓展

1. Introduction of South Korean Economy

South Korea is one of the wealthiest nations in the world with an economy that ranks 13th in by nominal GDP and 30th by purchasing power parity. It is a member of the Organization for Economic Co-operation and Development (OECD) and the G – 20, and is the only developed country in the group of Next Eleven countries.

South Korea's economy heavily relies on imports since it has few natural resources and suffers from overpopulation, which has forced South Korea to import a great deal of its basic needs and raw materials and to use these to produce finished goods for export. As a result, in 2012, South Korea was the seventh largest exporter and importer in the world.

Largely driven by export, South Korea's economy experience a rapid expansion through the last decades of the 20th century which relied heavily on an outward-facing economic policy that it continues to follow to this day. Best known for its cars and electronics, South Korea is also a dominant force in the world's shipbuilding. In fact, it controlled 50.6 percent of the global market for shipbuilding in 2008. Technology and telecommunications make up the largest portion of South Korea's export products, followed closely by automobiles. Refined petroleum, arms, mining, construction, and tourism make up other large portions of the economy.

South Korea's economy contracted following the global recession in 2008. Nevertheless, it was able to avoid a deep recession thanks to timely stimulus measures and strong domestic consumption of products that offset losses in exports.

2. FTA Linking China & South Korea More Closely

It is widely anticipated that the free trade agreement (FTA) between China and South

Korea will provide opportunity for the two countries to push forward their already-close cooperation partnership further.

Many experts believe that the free trade accord will help expand presence of South Korean companies in the world's largest consumer market and boost bilateral relations in trade and economy. China is South Korea's largest trading partner and South Korea stands as China's third-biggest single-country partner of trade. Within 20 years after the implementation, both countries will eliminate tariff on more than 90 percent of traded goods. South Korean companies are expected to reduce tariff costs by up to 5.44 billion dollars annually, much higher than tariff savings of 930 million dollars from the South Korea-U.S. FTA and 1.38 billion dollars from the South Korea-EU FTA. According to Seoul's estimates, South Korean manufacturers are forecast to see exports to China grow 1.35 billion U.S. dollars thanks to the implemented FTA within a year. South Korea expected the FTA with China to help raise its real GDP by 0.96 percentage points, create 53800 jobs and enhance consumer benefits by 14.6 billion dollars.

The China-South Korea trade deal will not only serve as growth engines for the two sides, deepening economic and trade cooperation further, but also play a role as a good starting point that will speed up negotiations on the trilateral FTA, also including Japan, and boost negotiations on the Regional Comprehensive Economic Partnership. China, South Korea and Japan, whose combined GDP makes up 20 percent of the world total, constitutes one of the three largest economic blocks worldwide, along with the European Union and North America.

案例 4　从日本 Yamanitzu 公司进口高级彩色复印机

商业背景设定：

进口商：广州诚亚文化用品公司（Guangzhou Chengya Stationary Commodity Co.,），公司批发各种文化用品，其销售渠道覆盖了整个华南市场。

公司地址：中国广东省广州市东兴路 66 号
总经理：赵刚
主要产品：文具

出口商：Yamanitzu 公司，日本著名的复印机设备生产商，其产品品质优良，价格合理，畅销世界多国市场。

公司地址：Room 546, Ninco Building, Ginzo, Tokyo
总经理：田中义一（Nakata Keyici）

近年来，中国文化产业市场繁荣发展，对于高端彩色复印机需求不断增加。诚亚公司将其定位为公司新的利润增长点，并决定利用自己的渠道优势，尽快占领市场。

诚亚公司经过长期的市场调查，认为 Yamanitzu 公司所生产的高级彩色复印机技术先进，具备较高知名度，非常符合其业务拓展的需要，因此希望能与 Yamanitzu 公司建立合作关系。

学习情境 1：建交函
(Correspondence for Establishing Business Relations)

知识目标： 1. 全面掌握建交函写作的要领。
2. 学习建交函写作的常用词组、典型句式。
3. 学习建交函写作的专业术语。
4. 学习建交函写作的商务背景知识。

能力目标： 1. 能够熟练运用本环节所学习的专业术语、常用词组、典型句式正确撰写建交函。
2. 掌握建交函写作所需要的相关商务背景知识。

任务： 诚亚公司总经理赵刚给 Yamanitzu 公司总经理 Nakata 先生发出一封建交函，表达与对方合作的意愿，并且希望早日得到回复。

请就此撰写一封建交函。

要求如下：

1. 介绍本公司基本情况。
2. 表达合作意愿。

你可以借助资料库中的相关资料来撰写建交函。

范例：

Dear Mr. Nakata,

We got your information from your website and understand you are the leading producer of color copier. As one of the biggest stationery commodity enterprises in China, our sales channels have covered the whole South China area. Now we are targeting at the high end color copier market and believe this goal can be achieved successfully by our joint efforts.

Should you require any further details about our company, please be free to let us know.

We are looking forward to hearing from you soon.

Sincerely yours

Zhao Gang

General Manager

学习情境2：询盘函（Correspondence for Enquiry）

知识目标： 1. 全面掌握询盘函写作的要领。
2. 学习询盘函的常用词组、典型句式。

3. 学习询盘函写作的专业术语。
4. 学习询盘函写作的商务背景知识。

能力目标： 1. 能够熟练运用本环节所学习的专业术语、常用词组、典型句式正确撰写询盘函。
2. 掌握询盘函写作所需要的相关商务背景知识。

任务： Yamanitzu公司正在寻找进入中国市场的机会，因此非常重视诚亚公司建立贸易关系的来函。Yamanitzu公司经过研究，认为这家公司资源丰富、渠道覆盖面广，非常适合本公司的产品特性，相信双方的合作有助于早日进入蓬勃发展的中国市场，因此决定和诚亚公司进行贸易联系。Nakata先生回函赵刚总经理，感谢诚亚公司的来信，并提出愿意给诚亚公司寄送样品以供其调研。

请就此撰写一封要求寄送样品的询盘函。

要求如下：
1. 感谢对方来电，表明公司希望双方能够紧密合作。
2. 承诺寄送最新研制的SKY-009彩色复印机2台。

你可以借助资料库中的相关资料来撰写询盘函。

范例：

Dear Mr. Zhao,

Your letter has been received with many thanks and we are happy to establish close business partnership with you.

We can provide you with our highest quality products and believe they will be welcomed by your customers. We have decide to send you 2 units of our latest model of SKY-009 Color Copier for your research.

Your favorable reply is awaited.

Sincerely yours

Nakata

任务： 诚亚公司收到 Yamanitzu 公司的回复函和随信寄送的样品，经过检验证明这些产品完全符合公司的预期，决定与其正式开始进口业务的磋商。赵刚总经理致函 Nakata 先生，告知对方计划首批订购 SKY-009 彩色复印机 100 台，要求对该批货物报价。

请就此撰写一封要求报价的询盘函。

要求如下：

1. 对寄送样品表示满意，表示要订购 SKY-009 彩色复印机 100 台。
2. 请求报 CIF 广州价。

你可以借助资料库中的相关资料来撰写询盘函。

范例：

Dear Mr. Nakata,

Thank you for your prompt reply and your samples have also been received with many thanks. The quality of your products proved to be very satisfying and we are sure our customers will like them, too.

Please let us know your lowest possible price for the relevant goods and for the first order, we would rather you quote us CIF Guangzhou for 100 units SKY-009 Color Copier.

If your price is competitive, we shall place order right away.

We are awaiting your early reply.

Sincerely yours

Zhao Gang

学习情境 3：发盘函（Correspondence for Offers）

知识目标： 1. 全面掌握发盘函写作的要领。

2. 学习发盘函写作的常用词组、典型句式。

3. 学习发盘函写作的专业术语。
4. 学习发盘函写作的商务背景知识。

能力目标： 1. 能够熟练运用本环节所学习的专业术语、常用词组、典型句式正确撰写发盘函。
2. 掌握发盘函写作所需要的相关商务背景知识。

任务： Yamanitzu 收到了诚亚公司的询盘函，很快就向其发出了详细的实盘。请就此撰写一封发盘函。
要求如下：
品名：SKY-009 彩色复印机
价格：CIF 广州价，每台 2000 美元
数量：100 台
包装：10 台装 1 木箱，10 箱装一个集装箱
交货期：收到信用证后 4 周内发货
保险：由卖方投保
支付方式：保兑的、不可撤销见票即付信用证
发盘有效期为 4 周

你可以借助资料库中的相关资料来撰写发盘函。

范例：

Dear Mr. Zhao,

Thank you for your prompt reply and kind enquiry and we are pleased to quote as follows.

Commodity：SKY-009 Color Copier
Price：CIF Guangzhou US＄2000 per unit
Quantity：100 units
Packing：Every 10 units in a wooden case, 10 cases in a FCL container
Delivery：within 4 weeks of receiving L/C
Term of Payment：by confirmed, irrevocable L/C at sight

案例 4　从日本 Yamanitzu 公司进口高级彩色复印机

Considering the fast increasing demand of this model, we can only keep the offer valid for 4 weeks.

We are looking forward to your favorable decision.

Yours faithfully

Nakata

学习情境 4：还盘函（Correspondence for Counter-offers）

知识目标： 1. 全面掌握还盘函写作的要领。
2. 学习还盘函写作的常用词组、典型句式。
3. 学习还盘函写作的专业术语。
4. 学习还盘函写作的商务背景知识。

能力目标： 1. 能够熟练运用本环节所学习的专业术语、常用词组、典型句式正确撰写还盘函。
2. 掌握还盘函写作所需要的相关商务背景知识。

任务： 诚亚公司收到报价后，经过测算，认为中国消费者对于该产品并不熟悉，这样高的价格肯定会影响其消费意愿，因此希望对方降低价格。
请就此撰写一封还盘函。
要求如下：
1. 告知报价偏高。
2. 希望价格降到 1700 美元/台。

你可以借助资料库中的相关资料来撰写还盘函。

范例：

Dear Mr. Nakata,

Your quote for SKY – 009 Color Copier has been received with many thanks. However, we regret to inform you that although your products are good in quality, we cannot place an order at this price because most of our customers are not familiar with your company and this price will considerably hamper their consumption intention.

In view of the long term development of our cooperation, we suggest that you lower your price to US $ 1700/unit, which we believe is a realistic and mutually beneficial offer.

Your favorable reply is anticipated.

Yours faithfully

Zhao Gang

学习情境5：订单函（Correspondence for Orders）

知识目标：1. 全面掌握订单函写作的要领。
2. 学习订单函写作的常用词组、典型句式。
3. 学习订单函写作的专业术语。
4. 学习订单函写作的商务背景知识。

能力目标：1. 能够熟练运用本环节所学习的专业术语、常用词组、典型句式正确撰写订单函。
2. 掌握订单函写作所需要的相关商务背景知识。

任务：经过双方多次协商，Yamanitzu接受了诚亚公司的还价，将价格下调至1700美元/台。诚亚公司向其下了订单。

请就此撰写一封订单函。
要求如下：
品名：SKY-009彩色复印机
价格：CIF广州价，每台1700美元
数量：100台
包装：10台装1木箱，10箱装一个集装箱
交货期：收到信用证后4周内发货
保险：由卖方投保
支付方式：保兑的、不可撤销见票即付信用证

你可以借助资料库中的相关资料来撰写订单函。

范例：

Dear Mr. Nakata,

We are pleased to enter the business with you finally and our order for SKY – 009 Color Copier is as follows.

Commodity：SKY – 009 Color Copier
  Price：US $ 1700 per unit CIF Guangzhou
  Quantity：100 units
  Packing：Every 10 in a wooden case, 10 cases in a FCL container
  Delivery：within 4 weeks of receiving L/C
  Term of Payment：by confirmed, irrevocable L/C at sight

We hope this deal will be the beginning of more and regular orders.

Sincerely yours

Zhao Gang

学习情境6：支付方式函（Correspondence for Term of Payment）

知识目标：1. 全面掌握支付方式函写作的要领。
    2. 学习支付方式函写作的常用词组、典型句式。
    3. 学习支付方式函写作的专业术语。
    4. 学习支付方式函写作的商务背景知识。
能力目标：1. 能够熟练运用本环节所学习的专业术语、常用词组、典型句式正确撰写支付方式函。
    2. 掌握支付方式函写作所需要的相关商务背景知识。

任务：Yamanitzu 公司收到了诚亚公司开立的信用证，审证时发现信用证与销售合同的条款有不符之处，因此致函要求修改。

请就此撰写一封信用证修改的通知函。

要求如下：

1. 说明信用证与合同有不符之处。
2. 要求将报价由 CIF 常州改为 CIF 广州。
3. 指出信用证应为不可撤销信用证。

你可以借助资料库中的相关资料来撰写更改支付方式请求函。

范例：

Dear Mr. Zhao,

We have received your L/C and found two discrepancies. Please make the following amendments:

1. "CIF Changzhou" should be "CIF Guangzhou"
2. The L/C should be "confirmed and irrevocable" instead of "irrevocable"

We are grateful if you could kindly consider this request.

Sincerely yours

Nakata

常用付款方式的风险分析：

T/T（Telegraphic Transfer）：电汇。这种结算方式一般指签订合同后，进口商支付定金。出口商在生产完毕后通知进口商付款，收到余款后发货，交付全套单证。出口商一般会要求收取 30% 或者更高比例的保证金或者预付款来提高交易的安全性。这样如果客户拒绝收货，可以在一定程度上减少材料及人工损失。

学习情境7：包装函（Correspondence for Packing）

知识目标：1. 全面掌握包装函写作的要领。
2. 学习包装函写作的常用词组、典型句式。

3. 学习包装函写作的专业术语。
4. 学习包装函写作的商务背景知识。

能力目标：1. 能够熟练运用本环节所学习的专业术语、常用词组、典型句式正确撰写包装函。
2. 掌握包装函写作所需要的相关商务背景知识。

任务：由于多次发生过商品运输途中受损的事件，诚亚公司专门致函 Yamanitzu 公司，强调务必按照要求对产品进行认真的包装。

请就此撰写一封包装指示函。

要求如下：
1. 要求将复印机用防水纸包裹后放置在木箱中，木箱应用防震海绵填塞
2. 集装箱外要标注"保持干燥"。

你可以借助资料库中的相关资料来撰写包装指示函。

范例：

Jun. 20, 2015

Dear Mr. Nakata,

We have experienced several accidents caused by poor packing and we consider it is necessary to reiterate the following instructions:

1. The copiers should be wrapped with waterproof paper before being placed in the wooden case which shall be filled up with sponge cushions.
2. The indicative mark of KEEP DRY should be shown clearly on the container.

We hope this issue can be handled with the utmost attention.

Yours sincerely,

Zhao Gang

学习情境 8：保险函（Correspondence for Insurance）

知识目标： 1. 全面掌握保险函写作的要领。
2. 学习保险函写作的常用词组、典型句式。
3. 学习保险函写作的专业术语。
4. 学习保险函写作的商务背景知识。

能力目标： 1. 能够熟练运用本环节所学习的专业术语、常用词组、典型句式正确撰写保险函。
2. 掌握保险函写作所需要的相关商务背景知识。

任务： 近期因海上天气变化较大，常常出现暴风雨，诚亚公司的多批货物在运输途中受损，因此致信 Yamanitzu 公司，要求其在合同约定的保险外，增加受热、受潮险。
请就此撰写一封要求卖方代为增加购买保险的请求函。
要求如下：
1. 请求诚亚公司按发票金额的 50% 增加受热、受潮险。
2. 承诺收到账单后会立即付还所垫付的保费。

你可以借助资料库中的相关资料来撰写保险函。

范例：

July 10, 2015

Dear Mr. Nakata

Due to the bad weather, several marine accidents have taken place recently which generated huge damage to our goods transported by ship. Therefore, we ask you to insure the consignment on our behalf against damage caused by heating & sweating for 50% of the invoice value. The refund of the premium will be made immediately upon receipt of your debit note.

Your approval would be highly appreciated.

案例 4 从日本 Yamanitzu 公司进口高级彩色复印机

Yours sincerely

Zhao Gang

学习情境 9：运输函（Correspondence for Shipment）

知识目标： 1. 全面掌握运输函写作的要领。
2. 学习运输函写作的常用词组、典型句式。
3. 学习运输函写作的专业术语。
4. 学习运输函写作的商务背景知识。

能力目标： 1. 能够熟练运用本环节所学习的专业术语、常用词组、典型句式正确撰写运输函。
2. 掌握运输函写作所需要的相关商务背景知识。

任务：诚亚公司按照合同规定，在货轮 Yosimoto 上预定了仓位。近期收到了轮船公司通知，Yosimoto 将在 12 月 10 日左右从东京港起航。公司给 Yamanitzu 发出了通知。
请就此撰写一封告知对方起运时间的通知函。
要求如下：
1. 告知对方起运时间。
2. 要求对方尽快完成装运工作。

你可以借助资料库中的相关资料来撰写通知函。

范例：

Dear Mr. Nakata

Our shipping company has just informed us that S/S Yosimoto will depart Tokyo Port around December 10.

We hope you can arrange the shipment of the goods a. s. a. p.

Sincerely yours

Zhao Gang

学习情境10：索赔和纠纷解决
(Correspondence for Claim and Settlement)

知识目标： 1. 全面掌握索赔函写作的要领。
2. 学习索赔函写作的常用词组、典型句式。
3. 学习索赔函写作的专业术语。
4. 学习索赔函写作的商务背景知识。

能力目标： 1. 能够熟练运用本环节所学习的专业术语、常用词组、典型句式正确撰写索赔函。
2. 掌握索赔函写作所需要的相关商务背景知识。

任务： Yosimoto货轮抵达广州后，诚亚公司对货品进行了验收，发现10台复印机包装不善导致零件生锈，提出索赔。

请就此撰写一封索赔函。

要求如下：
1. 告知货物已收到。
2. 告知对方10台复印机包装不善导致零件生锈，提出索赔2万美元。

你可以借助资料库中的相关资料来撰写索赔函。

范例：

Dear Mr. Nakata,

We are sorry to inform you that the inspection of the goods found 10 copiers were damaged due to poor packing, which no doubt will affect our sales seriously as we have received the orders from our customers. We have to ask you to pay US $20000 for compensation.

We are looking forward to your reply.

Yours respectfully

Zhao Gang

案例4 从日本Yamanitzu公司进口高级彩色复印机

商业背景知识拓展

1. Introduction of Japanese Economy

In 2013, Japan was the third largest economy in the world and the second largest developed economy overall. Japan is a member of the Asia-Pacific Economic Cooperation (APEC), the World Trade Organization (WTO), the Organization for Economic Co-operation and Development (OECD), G-20, G8, and several others.

Japan lacks the natural resources to support its growing economy, it, therefore, exports goods in which it has a comparative advantage—such as high-tech products—to get raw materials and petroleum. While lacking in resources, Japan has become one of the largest processors of raw materials imported from abroad, relying on a strong infrastructure and highly skilled workforce.

Services account for the bulk of Japan's economy, employing about 68.9 percent of the population. Finance is one of the biggest services in Japan, with the Tokyo Stock Exchange being the world's fourth largest stock market. Japan runs an annual trade surplus and has a considerable net international investment surplus, which makes it second largest holder of private financial assets in the world. 62 of the Fortune Global 500 companies base themselves in Japan.

While the Japanese economy has rebounded from the global recession, that recovery has been slower than in some other nations. In 2015, the Japan experienced an economic growth of just 0.9 percent. Inflation, on the other hand, continues to hover at around 3.2 percent. Nevertheless, rising wages and declining unemployment point to strong growth in 2015, and consumer confidence appears to be on the rise, as well. Low oil prices and a weakened yen have also helped Japan's export industries.

The biggest problem threatening Japan's future prosperity is there has been little progress in implementing several pro-growth reforms, which has led to some uncertainty among foreign investors, who remain reluctant to invest too heavily.

2. China and Japan Sitting on the Same Boat

For years, Japan has been China's single largest source of imports. About 60 – 70 percent of the goods China imports from Japan are the machinery and parts needed to make China's own products. According to a 2012 International Monetary Fund report, for every one percent of growth in China's global exports, its imports from Japan rise by 1.2 percent.

Take the iPhone and the iPad as an example. SKY – 009 Color Copier hires Foxconn from Taiwan Province to assemble the products, but the key parts come from Japan, including Toshiba flash memory drives and Sharp LCD screens. This example is instructive for two reasons. First, as China has increasingly begun to export high-tech products, it has needed to rely more and more on imported parts. And it is precisely these import-intensive machinery and electronics products that are becoming more important to China's economy. Second, China's modernization depends on a host of multinational corporations using China as their workshop. These companies rely on imports from Japan. China cannot single out Japanese products without damaging and alienating the network of multinational companies that are fueling China's march up the value chain and toward higher living standards.

Today, China's cheap but high-quality labor and its fantastic infrastructure make the country an attractive production base. But as long as multinationals want to assemble products in China, Japanese suppliers need to be there. What is more, China's bulging middle-class market is too big to be ignored by Japanese companies that produce consumer products and are plagued by low growth at home. Indeed, in a survey conducted by the Japan External Trade Organization, 52 percent of Japanese companies in China said they planned on expanding. In 2012, a year in which global foreign direct investment in China fell by 3.7 percent, Japanese investment rose by 6 percent.

案例 5　从德国 Gutenberg 公司进口汽车发动机

商业背景设定：
进口商：北京风驰特种车辆有限公司（Beijing Fengchi Special Vehicle Company），中国最大的特种车辆制造企业之一，技术力量雄厚，在特种车辆研发、外观设计、售后服务等方面均有良好的口碑。

公司地址：中国北京经济开发区博大路 5 号
总经理：赵越
主要产品：特种车辆

出口商：Gutenberg 公司系德国知名的特种车辆进口和销售商，其营销网络覆盖了德国、泰国、马来西亚、越南等国家，年营业额超过 20 亿美元。

公司地址：500Von Rohen Street, Berlin
总经理：Von Brecht

风驰公司的产品在中国及周边市场具有较高的知名度和市场份额，目前正在积极进入中东市场。风驰公司根据中东客户的需求，开发研制了一款全地形车。由于中东客商对车辆的速度有较高的要求，公司研发部门建议配备德国 Gutenberg 公司生产的 KKF – 135 柴油发动机。

学习情境 1：建交函
(Correspondence for Establishing Business Relations)

知识目标： 1. 全面掌握建交函写作的要领。
2. 学习建交函写作的常用词组、典型句式。
3. 学习建交函写作的专业术语。
4. 学习建交函写作的商务背景知识。

能力目标： 1. 能够熟练运用本环节所学习的专业术语、常用词组、典型句式正确撰写建交函。
2. 掌握建交函写作所需要的相关商务背景知识。

任务：风驰公司总经理赵越给 Gutenberg 公司总经理 Brecht 先生发出一封建交函，表达与对方合作的意愿，并且希望早日得到回复。

请就此撰写一封建交函。

要求如下：

1. 介绍本公司基本情况。
2. 表达合作意愿。

你可以借助资料库中的相关资料来撰写建交函。

范例：

Fengchi Company
No. 5 Boda Road,
BDA, Beijing
P. R. China
Mar. 20, 2016

Gutenberg
500 Von Rohen Street
Berlin, Germany

Dear Mr. Brecht,

We learn from the German Commercial Chamber in Beijing that you are the leading manufacturer of the diesel engine in Germany.

We have the pleasure to introduce our company to you in the hope of establishing business relations with you. As one of the biggest special vehicle producers in China, we are developing a new ATV which targets at the Middle East market. Our engineers believe your KKF-135 engine is an ideal engine for our product. We are sure if we work together, both of our companies will have a great opportunity for development.

Please contact us if you are interested in this proposal.

We are looking forward to hearing from you soon.

Sincerely yours

Zhao Yue

General Manager

学习情境2：询盘函（Correspondence for Enquiry）

知识目标：1. 全面掌握询盘函写作的要领。
2. 学习询盘函的常用词组、典型句式。
3. 学习询盘函写作的专业术语。
4. 学习询盘函写作的商务背景知识。

能力目标：1. 能够熟练运用本环节所学习的专业术语、常用词组、典型句式正确撰写询盘函。
2. 掌握询盘函写作所需要的相关商务背景知识。

任务：Gutenberg公司正在积极准备大规模进入中国市场，因此非常重视风驰公司的商业建议。Gutenberg公司通过德国商会得知风驰公司是一家实力雄厚的中国企业，有较高的信用度。经过董事会研究，决定和风驰公司进行贸易联系。Brecht先生回函赵越总经理，感谢风驰公司的来信，愿意与之进行合作并且邀请风驰公司尽快派遣商务和技术人员来公司考察。

请就此撰写一封要求寄送样品的询盘函。

要求如下：

1. 感谢对方来电，表明公司希望双方能够紧密合作。
2. 邀请风驰公司派遣商务和技术人员来公司考察。

你可以借助资料库中的相关资料来撰写询盘函。

范例：

Dear Mr. Zhao,

Thank you for your business proposals and we are very impressed by your sincerity and strategic vision.

Our board has made the decision to cooperate with you and we hope you can send your commercial and technical teams to our company, which will, we are confident generate mutually beneficial results.

We await your prompt reply.

Sincerely yours

Brecht

President

任务：风驰公司迅速派遣相关团队去 Gutenberg 公司进行考察，认为其产品质量和生产能力均符合公司的要求与标准，可以满足中东消费者的需求。赵越总经理致函 Brecht 先生，告知对方计划订购 KKF-135 柴油发动机 1000 台，要求对该批货物报价。
请就此撰写一封要求报价的询盘函。
要求如下：
1. 对寄送样品表示满意，要订购 1000 台 KKF-135 柴油发动机。
2. 请求报 CIF 天津价。

你可以借助资料库中的相关资料来撰写询盘函。

范例：

Dear Mr. Brecht,

Our delegate submitted to our board a report on your company, which highly evaluates your product of KKF-135 and production capacity. We believe this engine can match our newest ATV perfectly.

Please quote us your lowest possible CIF Tianjing price for 1000 engines. The order will be placed if your price is reasonable.

Your early reply is highly appreciated.

Sincerely yours

Zhao Yue

学习情境3：发盘函（Correspondence for Offers）

知识目标： 1. 全面掌握发盘函写作的要领。
2. 学习发盘函写作的常用词组、典型句式。
3. 学习发盘函写作的专业术语。
4. 学习发盘函写作的商务背景知识。

能力目标： 1. 能够熟练运用本环节所学习的专业术语、常用词组、典型句式正确撰写发盘函。
2. 掌握发盘函写作所需要的相关商务背景知识。

任务： Gutenberg公司收到风驰公司的询盘函，经过认真的研究，很快向风驰公司发盘。请就此撰写一封发盘函。

要求如下：

品名：KKF-135柴油发动机

价格：CIF天津价，每台3000美元

数量：1000台

包装：10台装1木箱

交货期：2016年6月

支付方式：不可撤销即期汇票信用证

你可以借助资料库中的相关资料来撰写发盘函。

范例：

Dear Mr. Zhao,

We are very glad to know that our product satisfies your demands and We are pleased to quote as follows.

Commodity: KKF – 135 Engine
Price: US $ 3000 per set, CIF Tianjin
Quantity: 1000 sets
Packing: 10 sets in a wooden case
Shipment: June, 2016
Payment: by irrevocable L/C, payable by draft at sight

We believe this price is very competitive and are looking forward to your favorable reply.

Yours faithfully

Von Brecht

学习情境4：还盘函（Correspondence for Counter-offers）

知识目标：1. 全面掌握还盘函写作的要领。
2. 学习还盘函写作的常用词组、典型句式。
3. 学习还盘函写作的专业术语。
4. 学习还盘函写作的商务背景知识。

能力目标：1. 能够熟练运用本环节所学习的专业术语、常用词组、典型句式正确撰写还盘函。
2. 掌握还盘函写作所需要的相关商务背景知识。

任务：风驰公司收到报价后，经测算发现，如果按Gutenberg公司当前的报价，其特种车辆的最终定价将会超过原计划，很可能会影响消费者的购买意愿，因此致函Brecht先生，希望对方能适当降低价格。

请就此撰写一封还盘函。

要求如下：

1. 告知Gutenberg公司认为报价偏高。
2. 希望价格能降到2500美元/台。

你可以借助资料库中的相关资料来撰写还盘函。

范例：

案例5　从德国Gutenberg公司进口汽车发动机

Dear Mr. Brecht,

Your offer for KKF – 135 Engine has been received with many thanks. However, we found it beyond our expectation and if we accept this quote, the final price of our ATV will be too high to be competitive on the Middle East market. A lower price will attract more customers and this is helpful to win the market for your product in the long run. Therefore, we would like to place an order with you if you could reduce your price to US $ 2500 per set.

Your prompt reply will be appreciated.

Yours faithfully

Zhao Yue

学习情境5：订单函（Correspondence for Orders）

知识目标：1. 全面掌握订单函写作的要领。
2. 学习订单函写作的常用词组、典型句式。
3. 学习订单函写作的专业术语。
4. 学习订单函写作的商务背景知识。

能力目标：1. 能够熟练运用本环节所学习的专业术语、常用词组、典型句式正确撰写订单函。
2. 掌握订单函写作所需要的相关商务背景知识。

任务：经过双方多次协商，Gutenberg公司最终接受了风驰公司的要求，将价格下调至2500美元。风驰公司向其下订单。

请就此撰写一封订单函。

要求如下：

品名：KKF – 135 柴油发动机

价格：CIF 天津价，每台2500美元

数量：1000 台

包装：10 台装1木箱

交货期：2016 年 6 月

支付方式：不可撤销即期汇票信用证

你可以借助资料库中的相关资料来撰写订单函。

范例：

Dear Mr. Brecht,

We are pleased to order with you 1000 sets of KKF – 135 Engine and our order is as follows.

> Commodity：KKF – 135 Diesel Engine
> Price：US＄2500 per set，CIF Tianjin
> Quantity：1000 sets
> Packing：10 sets in a wooden box
> Shipment：June, 2016
> Payment：by irrevocable L/C, payable by draft at sight

If the first order proves successful, we will place larger orders in the near future.

Sincerely yours

Zhao Yue

学习情境6：支付方式函（Correspondence for Term of Payment）

知识目标：1. 全面掌握支付方式函写作的要领。
　　　　　2. 学习支付方式函写作的常用词组、典型句式。
　　　　　3. 学习支付方式函写作的专业术语。
　　　　　4. 学习支付方式函写作的商务背景知识。

能力目标：1. 能够熟练运用本环节所学习的专业术语、常用词组、典型句式正确撰写支付方式函。
　　　　　2. 掌握支付方式函写作所需要的相关商务背景知识。

任务：按照双方签署的销售合同，风驰公司应该在4月10日之前将其在银行开立信用证寄送至 Gutenberg 公司，但是直到4月25日，Gutenberg 公司仍然没有收到信用证。

请就此撰写一封催促开立信用证通知函。

要求如下：

1. 告知本公司尚未收到应该在4月10日前寄送到达的信用证。
2. 提请尽快开立信用证，否则会影响装运时间。

你可以借助资料库中的相关资料来撰写开立信用证通知函。

范例：

Dear Mr. Zhao

Subject：Establishment of L/C for KKF – 135 Engine

We have not receive your L/C against our order of KKF – 135 Engine, which according to the sales contract should have reached us by April 10.

The time of shipment will be delayed if you do not send the L/C concerned to us before the end of this month.

Yours faithfully

Von Brecht

学习情境7：包装函（Correspondence for Packing）

知识目标：1. 全面掌握包装函写作的要领。
2. 学习包装函写作的常用词组、典型句式。
3. 学习包装函写作的专业术语。
4. 学习包装函写作的商务背景知识。

能力目标：1. 能够熟练运用本环节所学习的专业术语、常用词组、典型句式正确撰写包装函。
2. 掌握包装函写作所需要的相关商务背景知识。

任务：Gutenberg 公司按照合同要求在"Goldberg"号货轮上预订好舱位后通知风驰公司。风驰公司致信对方再次确认包装相关的条款和包装要求，强调务必按照要求对产品进行认真的包装。

请就此撰写一封包装指示函。

要求如下：
1. 要求发动机需用防水衬垫包裹。
2. 强调包装要防潮、防震。
3. 要求箱子的主标志需注明毛重、净重、目的港、原产国。

你可以借助资料库中的相关资料来撰写包装指示函。

范例：

Dear Mr. Brecht,

Thank you for booking space on S/S Goldberg for the goods and we consider it important and necessary to reiterate some of the packing requirements.

  1. The engines should be wrapped closely with anti-water cushions before being placed into the wooden box.
  2. The packing should be against moisture and shock.
  3. The main shipping mark should demonstrate the gross and net weight, port of destination and country of origin.

We look forward to hearing from you.

Yours sincerely,

Zhao Yue

学习情境8：保险函（Correspondence for Insurance）

  知识目标：1. 全面掌握保险函写作的要领。
               2. 学习保险函写作的常用词组、典型句式。

     3. 学习保险函写作的专业术语。
     4. 学习保险函写作的商务背景知识。
  能力目标：1. 能够熟练运用本环节所学习的专业术语、常用词组、典型句式正确撰写保险函。
     2. 掌握保险函写作所需要的相关商务背景知识。

  任务：按照合同要求，Gutenberg 公司应该为此货物购买保险，公司为此致电德意志保险公司，询问从汉堡港到天津港的保险费率。
  请就此撰写一封保险费率征询函。
  要求如下：
  1. 说明保险货物、货物价值、装运货轮、起止区间。
  2. 说明保险品种。

你可以借助资料库中的相关资料来撰写保险函。

范例：

Dear Sirs,

We are writing to inquire about your insurance rate as we are going to transport 1000 diesel engines from Hamburg to Tianjin Port of China. The goods are valued at US $2500000 and will be on S/S Goldberg before the end of July.

We should be pleased if you would quote us for All Risks as soon as possible.

Yours sincerely

Von Brecht

学习情境 9：运输函（Correspondence for Shipment）

  知识目标：1. 全面掌握运输函写作的要领。
     2. 学习运输函写作的常用词组、典型句式。
     3. 学习运输函写作的专业术语。
     4. 学习运输函写作的商务背景知识。

能力目标： 1. 能够熟练运用本环节所学习的专业术语、常用词组、典型句式正确撰写运输函。
2. 掌握运输函写作所需要的相关商务背景知识。

任务： Gutenberg 公司按照合同规定，准时将出口货物运送至汉堡港。在所有货物顺利装运上 "Goldberg" 号货轮后，Brecht 先生致信赵越总经理，告知其装运完毕，并且附上装运单据。

请就此撰写一封告知对方装运完成的通知函。

要求如下：

1. 告知对方启运时间是在 7 月 20 日左右。
2. 告知对方随函附上装运单据，其中包括不可转让提单、签署好的发票、装箱单、原产地证明、保险单等。

你可以借助资料库中的相关资料来撰写通知函。

范例：

Dear Mr. Zhao,

We are pleased to inform you that the shipment has been finished on July 19 on S/S Goldberg at Hamburg Port which is due to leave for Tianjin on or about July 20.

Enclosed kindly find the duplicate shipping documents which include:
    a. A non-negotiable copy of bill of lading
    b. A signed invoice
    c. Packing list
    d. Certificate of Origin
    e. Insurance policy

We are happy to have filled your order on time and sure the goods will you're your demands.

Sincerely yours

Von Brecht

学习情境10：索赔和纠纷解决
(Correspondence for Claim and Settlement)

知识目标： 1. 全面掌握索赔函写作的要领。
2. 学习索赔函写作的常用词组、典型句式。
3. 学习索赔函写作的专业术语。
4. 学习索赔函写作的商务背景知识。

能力目标： 1. 能够熟练运用本环节所学习的专业术语、常用词组、典型句式正确撰写索赔函。
2. 掌握索赔函写作所需要的相关商务背景知识。

任务： 两个月后，风驰公司收到了订购的发动机。但是在验收货物时，发现少运了50台，因此向 Gutenberg 公司提出索赔。Gutenberg 公司经过调查，证明已经按照合同要求将1000台发动机装箱并装运上货轮，因此对于货物的缺失不应承担任何责任。

请就此撰写一封索赔回复函。

要求如下：

1. 告知风驰公司，经过公司调查，装运的发动机数量与合同完全相符。
2. 建议对方向轮船公司或者保险公司联系赔偿事宜。

你可以借助资料库中的相关资料来撰写索赔回复函。

范例：

Dear Mr. Zhao,

We conducted a serious investigation immediately after receiving your letter, which shows that the number of engine we sent to the ship was in strict accordance with the number in the contract. Therefore, the shortage must have happened during the transit, for which we should not be held responsible.

We advise you to contact the transporter or insurance company for compensation.

Sincerely yours

Von Brecht

商业背景知识拓展

1. Introduction of German Economy

Germany is the largest economy in Europe and the fourth-largest in the world. Being a founding member of the European Union and the Eurozone, its economic model is based on the concept of the social market economy.

Germany recorded the highest trade surplus in the world in 2014, which made it the biggest capital exporter globally. Germany is the third largest exporter in goods and services. The service sector contributes around 70% of the total GDP, and exports account for 41% of national output. The top 10 exports of Germany are vehicles, machineries, chemical goods, electronic products, electrical equipment, pharmaceuticals, transport equipment, basic metals, food products, and rubber and plastics.

Germany is rich in iron, timber, nickel, copper and natural gas. 50% of energy in Germany is sourced by fossil fuels, followed by nuclear power, gas, wind, wood biofuels, hydro and solar. As the first major industrialized nation to commit to the renewable energy transition, Germany is the leading producer of wind turbines in the world. Renewables now produce over 27% of electricity consumed in Germany.

Small and medium-sized enterprises make up around 99 percent of all German companies, which are mostly family-owned. 53 of the world's 2000 largest publicly listed companies are headquartered in Germany. Germany is also the world's top location for trade fairs, where two thirds of the world's leading trade fairs take place.

2. Sino-German Trade

China replaced the USA as the world's top exporting nation in 2013 and sees Germany as its window to Europe. Germany counts as China's top trading partner in the Europe Union and ranks sixth in terms of global trading partners. China is Germany's top trading partner in Asia and third largest global trading partner.

Sino-German trade has increased dramatically in the last forty years. China is the fifth largest destination for German exports which include automobile and automobile parts, machines, data processing equipment, electrical and optical products, electrical equipment and chemical products. Chinese imports rank second amongst the products imported by Germany. The main products imported include data processing equipment, electrical and optical products, textiles and clothes, electronic equipment, machines and metal products. In 2013, bilateral trade between Germany and China amounted to over €140 billion.

German companies are becoming increasingly active in China. In 2013, German direct investments in China increased by almost 50%. More than 5000 German companies are currently active in China.

The 'Going Out Strategy' encourages Chinese companies to realize the potential of investing internationally. In 2013, Chinese direct investment in Germany amounted to around $2bn. Around 900 Chinese companies are active in Germany. Chinese investments in Germany mainly cover areas such as mechanical engineering, electronics, consumer goods, regenerative energy and information communication technologies.

资源库

资源库1　国际贸易常用保险简介

当前国际贸易货物的主要运送方式为海运、陆运、空运、邮政送递等。国际贸易货物保险也可以大致归纳为海洋运输货物保险、陆地运输货物保险、航空运输货物保险、邮包保险。

在国际货物买卖过程中，由哪一方负责办理投保，应根据买卖双方商订的价格条件来确定。例如按 F. O. B. 条件和 C. F. R. 条件成交，保险即应由买方办理；如按 C. I. F. 条件成交，保险就应由卖方办理。办理货运保险的一般程序是：确定投保的金额→填写投保单→支付保险费→取得保险单→提出索赔手续。索赔应当在保险有效期内提出并办理，否则保险公司可以不予办理。

一、海洋运输货物保险

主要险别

（1）平安险（Free From Particular Average，简称 F. P. A.）

责任范围主要包括：

a. 运输过程中，由于自然灾害和运输工具发生意外事件，被保险货物的实际全损或推定全损。

b. 由于运输工具遭搁浅、触礁、沉没、互撞、与其他物体碰撞以及失火、爆炸等意外事故造成被保险货物的部分损失。

c. 运输工具曾经发生搁浅、触礁、沉没、焚毁等意外事故，不论这事故发生之前或者以后曾在海上遭恶劣气候、雷电、海啸等自然灾害所造成的被保险货物的部分损失。

d. 在装卸转船过程中，被保险货物一件或数件落海所造成的全部损失或部分损失。

e. 运输工具遭自然灾害或意外事故，在避难港卸货所引起被保险货物的全部损失或部分损失。

f. 运输工具遭自然灾害或意外事故，需要在中途的港口或者在避难港口停靠，因而引起的卸货、装货、存仓以及运送货物所产生的特别费用。

　　g. 发生共同海损所引起的牺牲、公摊费和救助费用。

　　h. 发生了保险责任范围内的危险，被保险人对货物采取抢救、防止或少损失的各种措施，因而产生合理施救费用。但是保险公司承担费用的限额不能超过这批被救货物的保险金额。施救费用可以在赔款金额以外的一个保险金额限度内承担。

　　（2）水渍险（With Particular Average，简称 W. P. A.）

　　责任范围除"平安险"的责任外，还承担由于恶劣气候、雷电、海啸、地震、洪水等自然灾害所造成的保险货物部分损失。

　　（3）一切险（All Risks）

　　责任范围除"平安险"和"水渍险"的责任外，还包括货物在运输过程中，因各种外来原因所造成保险货物的损失。不论全损或部分损失，除对某些运输途耗的货物，经保险公司与被保险人双方约定在保险单上载明的免赔率外，保险公司都给予赔偿。

　　（4）附加险（Additronal risk）

　　附加险必须附着在主要险种下，不能单独购买。当前常用附加险有 11 种：

　　a. 偷窃提货不着险（Theft, Pilferage and Non-delivery Risk，简称 T. P. N. D.）：在保险有效期内，保险货物被偷窃，以及货物运抵目的地以后，整件未交的损失，保险公司负责赔偿。

　　b. 淡水雨淋险（Fresh Water Rain Damage，简称 F. W. R. D.）：货物在运输中，由于淡水、雨水以及雪溶所造成的损失，保险公司负责赔偿。

　　c. 短量险（Risk of Shortage）：负责保险货物数量短少和重量的损失。

　　d. 混杂、沾险（Risk of Intermixture & Contamination）：保险货物在运输过程中，混进了杂质所造成的损坏。

　　e. 渗漏险（Risk of Leakage）：流质、半流质的液体物质和油类物质，在运输过程中因为容器损坏而引起的渗漏损坏。

　　f. 碰损、破碎险（Risk of Clash & Breakage）：碰损主要是对金属、木质等货物来说的，破碎则主要是对易碎性物质来说的。前者是指在运输途中，因为受到震动、颠簸、挤压而造成货物本身的损失；后者是在运输途中由于装卸野蛮、粗鲁、运输工具的颠震造成货物本身的破裂、断碎的损失。

　　g. 串味险（Risk of Odor）：货物在运输途中受到一起堆储的其他货物所散发异味而导致品质受损。

　　h. 受热、受潮险（Damage Caused by Heating & Sweating）：船舶在航行途中，由于气温骤变，或者因为船上通风设备失灵等使舱内水汽凝结、发潮、发热引起货物的损失。

　　i. 钩损险（Hook Damage）：保险货物在装卸过程中因为使用手钩、吊钩等工具所造成的损失。

　　j. 包装破裂险（Loss for Damage by Breakage of Packing）：因为包装破裂造成物资的短少、玷污等损失。

　　k. 锈损险（Risk of Rust）：保险公司负责保险货物在运输过程中因为生锈造成的损失。

(5) 特别附加险（Spevial Extraneous risks）

特别附加险也属附加险类内，但不属于一切险的范围之内。它与政治、国家行政管理规章所引起的风险相关。例如战争险（War Risk）和罢工险（Strikes Risk）等。

二、陆上运输货物保险

陆上运输货物保险是货物运输保险的一种，分为陆运险和陆运一切险种。

1. 陆运险

责任范围包括被保险货物在运输途中遭受暴风、雷电、地震、洪水等自然灾害，或由于陆上运输工具（主要是指火车、汽车）遭受碰撞、倾覆或出轨而导致的损失。保险公司对陆运险的承保范围大至相当于海运险中的"水渍险"。

2. 陆运一切险

责任范围除包括陆运险的责任外，被保险货物在运输途中由于外来原因造成的短少、短量、偷窃、渗漏、碰损、破碎、钩损、雨淋、生锈、受潮、霉、串味等全部或部分损失。

3. 陆上运输货物保险的除外责任

（1）被保险人的故意行为或过失所造成的损失。

（2）属于发货人所负责任或被保险货物的自然消耗所引起的损失。

（3）由于战争、工人罢工或运输延迟所造成的损失。

三、航空运输货物保险（Air Transportation Cargo Insurance）

1. 航空运输险

被保险货物遭受损失时，按保险单上订明承保险别的条款负赔偿责任。

2. 航空运输一切险

除包括航空运输险责任外，对被保险货物在运输中由于外来原因造成的偷窃、短少等部分损失也负赔偿之责。

四、邮包保险

承保通过邮政局邮包寄递的货物在邮递过程中发生保险事故所致的损失。

以邮包方式将货物发送到目的地可能通过海运，也可能通过陆上或航空运输，或者经过两种或两种以上的运输工具运送。不论通过何种运送工具，凡是以邮包方式将贸易货物运达目的地的保险均属邮包保险。邮包保险按其保险责任分为邮包险（parcel post risks）和邮包一切险（parcel post all risks）两种。前者与海洋运输货物保险水渍险的责任相似，后者与海洋运输货物保险一切险的责任基本相同。

资源库 2 国际贸易常用报价与付款方式

一、国际贸易常用报价方式

报价方式	EXW	FOB	CIF	CFR
英文全名	Ex Works	Free on Board	Cost Insurance Freight	Cost Freight
中文名称	工厂交货价	离岸价	到岸价	成本加运费
交货地点	出口国工厂或仓库	卖方所在国装运港	买方所在国装运港	买方所在国装运港
运输	买方	买方	卖方	卖方
保险	买方	买方	卖方	买方
出口手续	买方	买方	卖方	卖方
进口手续	买方	卖方	卖方	买方
风险转移	交货地	装运港船舷	装运港船舷	装运港船舷
所有权转移	随买卖转移	随交单转移	随交单转移	随交单转移

二、国际贸易常用的付款方式

1. 信用证 L/C（Letter of Credit）

信用证是目前国际贸易付款方式最常用的一种方式。由银行担保付款，从理论上来说是非常保险的付款方式。

2. 电汇 T/T（Telegraphic Transfer）

电汇操作分为前 T/T 和后 T/T。

前 T/T：签订合同——买家付一部分定金（一般都是30%）——卖家生产完毕——通知买家付款——买家余款付清——卖家发货并交付全套单证。此方式对客户信誉度要求较高，因此在欧美国家出现的比较多。

后 T/T：签订合同——买家支付定金——卖家安排生产和出货——卖家寄送单证拷贝件——买家付余款——卖家收到余款后寄送全套单证。该方式国内较为常见。

3. D/P 付款交单（Documents Against Payment）

付款交单方式下，进口方付款后才能向代收银行领取单据。可分为即期交单（D/P at sight）和远期交单（D/P after sight or after date）。

即期交单：出口方开具即期汇票，由代收行向进口方提示，进口方见票后即须付款，货款付清时，进口方取得货运单据。

远期交单：出口方开具远期汇票，由代收行向进口方提示，经进口方承兑后，于汇票到期日或汇票到期日以前，进口方付款赎单。

4. D/A 承兑交单（Documents against Acceptance）

在跟单托收方式下，出口方（或代收银行）向进口方以承兑为条件交付单据的一种办法。

资源库3　国际贸易规范术语举要

BAF：燃油附加费 Bunker Adjustment Factor
B/L：海运提单 Bill of Lading
B/R：买价 Buying Rate
C&F：成本加海运费 Cost and Freight
CIF：成本，保险加海运费 Cost, Insurance, Freight
CPT：运费付至目的地 Carriage Paid To
CIP：运费、保险费付至目的地 Carriage and Insurance Paid To
C.Y.：货柜场 Container Yard
CFS：集装箱货运站 Cargo Freight Station
C/D：报关单 customs declaration
C.C：运费到付 Collect
CNTR NO.：柜号 Container Number
C.O：一般原产地证 Certificate of Origin
CTN/CTNS：纸箱 Carton/Cartons
C.S.C：货柜服务费 Container Service Charge
C/（CNEE）：收货人 Consignee
C/O：产地证 Certificate of Origin
CAF：货币汇率附加费 Currency Adjustment Factor
CFS：散货仓库 Container Freight Station
CHB：报关行 Customs House Broker
COMM：商品 Commodity
CTNR：柜子 Container
DAF：边境交货 Delivered At Frontier
DES：目的港船上交货 Delivered Ex Ship
DEQ：目的港码头交货 Delivered Ex Quay
DDU：未完税交货 Delivered Duty Unpaid
DDP：完税后交货 Delivered Duty Paid
DDC：目的港码头费 Destination Delivery Charge
DL/DLS：美元 dollar/dollars
D/P：付款交单 Document Against Payment
DOC：文件费 Document Charge

Doc#：文件号码 Document Number

D/A：承兑交单 Document Against Acceptance

DOZ/DZ：一打 Dozen

D/O：到港通知 Delivery Order

Ex：工厂交货 Work/ExFactory

ETA：到港日 Estimated Time of Arrival

ETD：开船日 Estimated Time of Delivery

ETC：截关日 Estimated Time of Closing

EXP：出口 Export

EA：每个，各 Each

EPS：设备位置附加费 Equipment Position Surcharges

FCA：货交承运人 Free Carrier

FOB：船上交货 Free On Board

FCL：整柜 Full Container Load

FCR：货物接收证明 Forward Cargo Receipt

FAF：燃料附加费 Fuel Adjustment Factor

F/F：货运代理 Freight Forwarder

FAK：各种货品 Freight All Kind

FAS：装运港船边交货 Free Alongside Ship

GRI：全面涨价 General Rate Increase

G.W.：毛重 Gross Weight

G.S.P.：普惠制 Generalized System of Preferences

HBL：货代提单 House Bill of Loading

H/C：代理费 Handling Charge

INT：国际的 International

INV：发票 Invoice

IMP：进口 Import

I/S：内销售 Inside Sales

IA：个别调价 Independent Action

LCL：拼柜 Less Than Container Load

L/C：信用证 Letter of Credit

LDP：完税交货价 Landed Duty Paid

MBL：主提单 Master Bill of Loading

M/V：商船 Merchant Vessel

MT：公吨 Metric Ton

M/T：尺码吨（即货物收费以尺码计费）Measurement Ton

MLB：小陆桥，自一港到另一港口 Mini Land Bridge

资源库3　国际贸易规范术语举要

MTD：多式联运单据 Multimodal Transport Document
NVOCC：无船承运人 Non Vessel Operating Common Carrier
N.W.：净重 Net Weight
N/F：通知人 Notify
O/F：海运费 Ocean Freight
OBL：海运提单 Ocean（or original）B/L
ORC：本地收货费用 Origen Receive Charges
OCP：货主自行安排运到内陆点 Overland Continental Point
OP：操作 Operation
POD：目的港 Port of Destination
POL：装运港 Port of Loading
PSS：旺季附加费 Peak Season Surcharges
REF：参考、查价 Reference
RMB：人民币 Renminbi
PRC：价格 Price
P/P：运费预付 Freight Prepaid
P.P：预付 Prepaid
PCS：港口拥挤附加费 Port Congestion Surcharge
PKG：一包，一捆，一扎，一件等 Package
PCE/PCS：只、个、支等 Piece/pieces
P/L：装箱单、明细表 Packing List
PCT：百分比 Percent
PUR：购买、购货 Purchase
S/O：装货指示书 Shipping Order
S/C：售货合同 Sales Contract
SC：服务合同 Service Contract
STL.：式样、款式、类型 Style
S.S：船运 Steamship
S/M：装船标记 Shipping Marks
S/R：卖价 Selling Rate
SSL：船公司 Steam Ship Line
SDR：特别提款权 Special drawing rights
T/T：电汇 Telegram Transit
T/T：航程 Transit Time
T.O.C：码头操作费 Terminal Operations Option
T.R.C：码头收柜费 Terminal Receiving Charge
T/S：转船，转运 Trans-Ship

TVC/ TVR：定期定量合同 Time Volume Contract/ Rate
TTL：总共 Total
VOCC：船公司 Vessel Operating Common Carrier
WT：重量 Weight
W/T：重量吨（即货物收费以重量计费）Weight Ton

资源库4 国际贸易重要港口要览

港口名称	国家与地区	港埠代码	中文名称
Abu Dhabi	阿联酋	AEAUH	阿布扎比
Adelaide	澳大利亚	AUADL	阿得雷德
Alexandria	埃及	EGALY	亚历山大
Amsterdam	荷兰	NLAMS	阿姆斯特丹
Antwerp	比利时	BEANR	安特卫普
Athens	希腊	GRATH	雅典
Atlanta	美国	USATL	亚特兰大
Auckland	新西兰	NZAKL	奥克兰
Baltimore	美国	USBAL	巴尔的摩
Bangkok	泰国	THBKK	曼谷
Barcelona	西班牙	ESBCN	巴塞罗那
Belawan	印度尼西亚	IDBLW	棉兰
Belfast	英国	GBBEL	贝尔法斯特
Birmingham	英国	GBBHX	伯明翰
Bombay	印度	INBOM	孟买
Boston	美国	USBOS	波士顿
Brisbane	澳大利亚	AUBNE	布里斯班
Bremerhaven	德国	DEBRV	不来梅哈文
Buenos aires	阿根廷	ARBUE	布宜诺斯艾利斯
Calcutta	印度	INCCU	加尔各答
Cape town	南非	ZACPT	开普敦
Charleston	美国	USCHS	查尔斯顿
Chiba	日本	JPCHB	千叶
Chicago	美国	USCHI	芝加哥
Chittagong	孟加拉	BDCGP	吉大
Christchurch	新西兰	NZCHC	基督城
Colombo	斯里兰卡	LKCMB	科伦坡

续表

港口名称	国家与地区	港埠代码	中文名称
Columbus	美国	USCMM	哥伦布
Copenhagen	丹麦	DKCPH	哥本哈根
Darwin	澳大利亚	AUDRW	达尔文
Detroit	美国	USDET	底特律
Dubai	阿联酋	AEDXB	迪拜
Dublin	爱尔兰	IEDUB	都柏林
Durban	南非	ZADUR	德班
Fos	法国	FRFOS	福斯
Glasgow	英国	GBGLW	格拉斯哥
Halifax	加拿大	CAHAL	哈利法克斯
Hamburg	德国	DEHAM	汉堡
Helsinki	芬兰	FIHEL	赫尔辛基
Hiroshima	日本	JPHIJ	广岛
Ho Chi Ming City	越南	VNSGN	胡志明市
Honolulu	美国	USHNL	檀香山
Houston	美国	USHOU	休斯敦
Incheon	韩国	KRINC	仁川
Jakarta	印度尼西亚	IDJKT	雅加达
Jeddah	沙特阿拉伯	SAJED	吉达
Kobe	日本	JPUKB	神户
Le havre	法国	FRLEH	哈里夫
Liverpool	英国	GBLIV	利物浦
London	英国	GBLON	伦敦
Long Beach	美国	USLGB	长滩
Los Angeles	美国	USLAX	洛杉矶
Lisbon	葡萄牙	PTLIS	里斯本
Marseilles	法国	FRMRS	马赛
Madras	印度	INMAA	马德拉斯
Melbourne	澳大利亚	AUMEL	墨尔本
Manchester	英国	GBMNC	曼彻斯特
Miami	美国	USMIA	迈阿密

资源库4 国际贸易重要港口要览

续表

港口名称	国家与地区	港埠代码	中文名称
Montreal	加拿大	CAMTR	蒙特利尔
Nagoya	日本	JPNGO	名古屋
New Orleans	美国	USNEW	新奥尔良
New York	美国	USNYC	纽约
Osaka	日本	JPOSA	大阪
Oslo	挪威	NOOSL	奥斯陆
Panama	巴拿马	PAPTY	巴拿马城
Philadelphia	美国	USPH	费城
Portland	美国	USPDX	波特兰
Pusan	韩国	KRPUS	釜山
Rotterdam	荷兰	NLRTM	鹿特丹
San Francisco	美国	USSFO	旧金山
Rio De Janeiro	巴西	BRRIO	里约热内卢
Sacramento	美国	USSAC	萨克拉门托
San Diego	美国	USSAN	圣地亚哥
Seattle	美国	USSEA	西雅图
Semarang	印度尼西亚	IDSRG	三宝垄
Stockholm	瑞典	SESTO	斯德哥尔摩
Stockton	美国	USSCK	斯托克顿
Sydney	澳大利亚	AUSYD	悉尼
Tampa	美国	USTPA	坦帕
Thames	英国	GBTHA	泰晤士港
Tokyo	日本	JPTYO	东京
Vancouver	加拿大	CAVAN	温哥华
Wellington	新西兰	NZWLG	惠林顿
Yokohama	日本	JPYOK	横滨

中国主要港口

港口名称	地区	港埠代码	中文名称
Dalian	中国大陆	CNDLC	大连
Fuzhou	中国大陆	CNFOC	福州
Guangzhou	中国大陆	CNCAN	广州

续表

港口名称	地区	港埠代码	中文名称
Haikou	中国大陆	CNHAK	海口
Hangzhou	中国大陆	CNHGH	杭州
Hong Kong	中国香港	HKHKG	香港
Hualien	中国台湾	TWHUN	花莲
Huangpu	中国大陆	CNHUA	黄埔
Jiang Men	中国大陆	CNJGM	江门
Keelung	中国台湾	TWKEL	基隆
Lianyungang	中国大陆	CNLYG	连云港
Nanjing	中国大陆	CNNKG	南京
Ningbo	中国大陆	CNNBO	宁波
Qingdao	中国大陆	CNTAO	青岛
Shanghai	中国大陆	CNSHA	上海
Shantou	中国大陆	CNSWA	汕头
Shekou	中国大陆	CNSKU	蛇口
Shenzhen	中国大陆	CNSZP	深圳
Taichung	中国台湾	TWTXG	台中
Wenzhou	中国大陆	CNWZH	温州
Xiamen	中国大陆	CNXMN	厦门
Xingang	中国大陆	CNNSK	天津新港
Zhanjiang	中国大陆	CNZHA	湛江

参考文献

1. 于翠萍，贝淑华，姜仕倩. 新编外贸英语函电 [M]. 南京：南京大学出版社，2015.
2. 肖艳. 外贸函电 [M]. 北京：北京大学出版社，2014.
3. 王晓俊. 外贸函电 [M]. 郑州：郑州大学出版社，2010.
4. 樊红霞，江莫才. 英文外贸函电 [M]. 北京：外语教学与研究出版社，2010.
5. 徐启华，朱传枝. 英语外贸函电 [M]. 沈阳：东北大学出版社，2009.
6. 赵立民. 外贸函电用语实用手册 [M]. 北京：对外经济贸易大学出版社，2009.
7. 蔡文芳. 外贸英语函电 [M]. 上海：上海交通大学出版社，2009.
8. 张耘. 纺织服装外贸函电与写作 [M]. 北京：中国纺织出版社，2008.
9. 冼燕华. 国际商务英语函电练习册及参考答案 [M]. 广州：暨南大学出版社，2008.
10. 尹小莹，杨润辉. 外贸英语函电：商务英语应用文写作 [M]. 西安交通大学出版社，2008.
11. Lin Lougheed. 实用商务函电写作 [M]. 上海：上海外语教育出版社，2008.
12. 凌芳. 商务英语函电模板手册 [M]. 北京：机械工业出版社，2008.